ROAD TRIP USA

Great River Road

Jamie Jensen

Contents

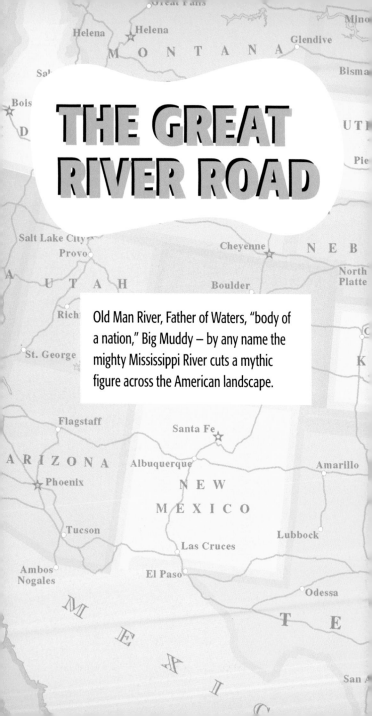

THE GREAT RIVER ROAD

Old Man River, Father of Waters, "body of a nation," Big Muddy — by any name the mighty Mississippi River cuts a mythic figure across the American landscape.

GRAND
FORKS

NORTH
DAKOTA

Bemidji

pg. 8

Mississippi
Headwaters

MN

Duluth

Mobridge

St. Cloud

WISCONS

Minneapolis

Paul

Green Bay

Oshkosh

World's Largest
Six-Pack

pg. 24

Crosse

Madison

Milwaukee

Sagin

DA

entine

Falls

Sioux City

Dubuque

Rockford

Lansing

SKA

Omaha

IOWA

Cedar
Rapids

Des
Moines

Lin

Mark Twain's
Hometown

pg. 48

Joseph

ILLIN

Springfield

C

Pe

Topeka

MISSOURI

Kansas
City

Jefferson City

St. Lou

Evan

N S A S

odge
City

Elvis Presley's
Graceland

Springfield

pg. 67

Ja

Nashville

TENNES

oma City

Fort
Smith

ARKANSAS

Chattanoog

KLAHOMA

Little Rock

Memphis

Hunt

Ardmore

Pine
Bluff

pg. 75

Greenda

Delta Blues
Museum

rt Worth

Dallas

Shreveport

Jackso

ne

Waco

OUISIANA

M

A   S

Lake

Baton R

Austin

Cajun Country

pg. 96

ew Orleans

Pensae

Housto

Lafayette

Galveston

Venice

SOUVENIR OF
LA CROSSE, WIS.

SACRED HEART

Between Lake Itasca, Minnesota, and the Gulf of Mexico

Old Man River, Father of Waters, "body of a nation," Big Muddy: By any name, the mighty Mississippi River cuts a mythic figure across the American landscape. Who hasn't read Mark Twain or listened to *Showboat* and not dreamed of a trip down the Mississippi? If you're tired of waiting for somebody to buy you passage aboard the *Delta Queen* or to help you paddle among the 1,500-ton barges, then do what Huck Finn would have done if he'd had a driver's license: Tag alongside the Mississippi on the Great River Road.

Created in 1938 from a network of federal, state, and local roads, the Great River Road—also known as the River Road, and commonly abbreviated to "GRR"—forms a single route along the Mississippi from head to toe. Designed to show off the 10 states bordering the Mississippi from its headwaters to its mouth, the GRR is nothing if not scenic, and anyone who equates the Midwest with the flat Kansas prairie will be pleasantly surprised. Sure, farms line the road, but so do upland meadows, cypress swamps, thick forests, limestone cliffs, and dozens of parks and wildlife refuges.

Of course it isn't all pretty. There's enough industry along the Mississippi for you to navigate the river by the flashing marker lights on smokestacks, and a half dozen major cities compete with their bigger cousins on the coasts for widest suburban sprawl and ugliest roadside clutter. A pandemic of tacky strip malls has infected the region, too, but apart from the astounding growth in casinos (you'll never be more than 100 miles from a slot machine from one end of the Mississippi to the other) the GRR resists the developers' bulldozers because its meanders are shunned by a century increasingly drawn to the straight, fast, and four-lane.

A full 50 percent longer than the comparable route along the Interstates, the GRR changes direction often, crosses the river whenever it can, dallies in towns every other road has forgotten, and altogether offers a perfect analog to floating downstream. If the road itself isn't your destination, *don't* take it. For those who do travel it, the GRR spares you the fleets of hurtling 40-ton trucks and that Interstate parade of franchised familiarity, and rewards you with twice the local color, flavor, and wildlife (two- and four-legged) found along any alternate route. Lest these tangibles be taken too much for granted, every so often the GRR will skip over to a freeway for a stretch to help you sort your preferences. Savor, and enjoy.

MINNESOTA

The Great River Road begins in **Lake Itasca State Park** and stair-steps along occasionally unpaved but well-graded backcountry roads through a mix of northern boreal forest, tree farms, and hayfields, all the while staying as close to its namesake as possible. By **Grand Rapids,** only 130 road miles from its source, the Mississippi has been transformed from a grassy brook barely deep enough to canoe to an indus-try-sustaining river fed by a half dozen of the state's 10,000 lakes. Farther south, the red and white pines, paper birch, and big-tooth aspen give way to more farms while the route breaks from the surveyor's section lines to curve with the river across

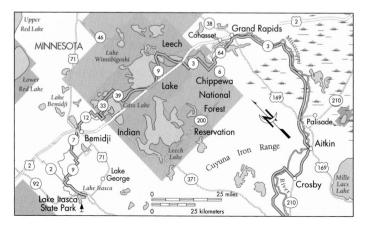

If the rivers were being named today, the Mississippi River would flow into the Missouri River and not vice versa, since the Missouri is by far the longer of the two.

the glacially flattened state. By **St. Cloud,** the GRR enters an increasingly developed corridor that culminates in the hugely sprawling Twin Cities of St. Paul and Minneapolis, south of which the road slips into rural Wisconsin.

Lake Itasca State Park

The GRR begins here among the cattails and tall pines, in the park that protects the **headwaters of the mighty Mississippi River.** The small, clear brook tumbling out of the north end of Lake Itasca will eventually carry runoff from nearly two-thirds of the United States and enough silt to make the muddy plume at the river's mouth visible from space. But at its headwaters, 2,550-odd meandering miles from the Gulf of Mexico, you can wade across the Mississippi, and the water is still so clean and clear you can see the bottom.

Throughout the upper Midwest, Friday night is the traditional night for a **fish fry.** Look for the backlit signboards or hand-lettered banners stuck out in front of the local VFW post or social club for a sample of the truly local variety.

The Mississippi's humble beginnings were the object of chest-thumping adventurers and the subject of not-so-scholarly debate for decades before explorer Henry Rowe Schoolcraft, led by Ojibwa native Ozaawindib, determined this lake to be the true source of the nation's most legendary river in 1832. Schoolcraft's story, the tale of the battle to protect the park against logging, and lots of other

Mississippi facts are found at the **interpretive center** just inside the park's north entrance (open year-round; $7 per car; 218/266-2114). Skeptics will also find out why professional geographers don't consider the two smaller lakes and the five creeks that feed Itasca competition for the headwaters title.

The fact that the lakeshore has been "improved" from its naturally marshy state, the surrounding old-growth pine forest—the most extensive stand of virgin timber left in the state—and outdoorsy amenities such as paved bike trails, boat launches, and newish café near the "official headwaters" all contribute to Itasca's popularity. Bike and boat rentals are available spring through fall opposite the park's headquarters.

Accommodations include the grand turn-of-the-20th-century **Douglas Lodge,** where rooms cost $70–115 a night, and assorted lakeside cabins (all overnight reservations can be made at 866/857-2757). Just steps from the bike path and beach

Navigating the Great River Road

The Great River Road (or GRR) is identified on signs by a green pilot's wheel with a steamboat pictured in the middle. Quality and quantity of route markers vary considerably from state to state; some states, like Minnesota and Illinois, are well marked, with advance warning of junctions and confirmation after turns, while other states, like Louisiana and Mississippi, seem committed to hiding GRR signs miles from where they would serve any conceivable good. Adding to the confusion are the many variations—signposted as Alternate or State Route—and spurs, denoted by a brown pilot's wheel, which lead off the GRR to various points of interest.

Though most people will be able to find their way along the riverside without too many dead-ends, trying to travel the length of the GRR just by following the signs is not recommended for perfectionists; part of the fun is getting slightly lost and making your own way. To ease your journey, get a detailed map of the entire GRR, and a guide to local happenings in each of the states along the route, from the **Mississippi River Parkway Commission**. Its very helpful, ad-free website is www.mississippiriverinfo.com.

you'll find the immaculate, friendly, and bargain-priced **HI Mississippi Headwaters Hostel** ($27 per person; 218/266-3415), which has rooms for families and couples as well as single travelers. When not fishing or foraging for your meals, consider the Douglas Lodge dining room, where the menu includes regional blueberries, wild rice, and walleye pike.

No matter when or how long you visit Lake Itasca, or anywhere in Minnesota really, be sure to pack plenty of potent repellent for ticks and mosquitoes.

Bemidji

Less than a century ago, the northern forests of Minnesota were chock-full of lumber boom camps, with hundreds of mills and lumber works whining night and day, and dozens of saloons,

Explorer Henry Schoolcraft christened Lake Itasca with syllables from the Latin *veritas caput,* meaning "true head."

It's a local legend that if you make a wish while stepping over Lake Itasca's Mississippi River headwaters, your wish will come true when the waters reach the Gulf of Mexico—about three months later.

brothels, and boardinghouses catering to the rough-and-tumble logging trade. The ravenous cutting wiped out the stands—virtually nothing remains of Minnesota's primeval pine forests—and the camps disappeared as quickly as they sprang up, but the woods have repeatedly grown back, to be harvested on a more sustainable basis while still providing an eye-pleasing backdrop to the region's literally thousands of lakes.

From its boomtown roots, **Bemidji** (pop. 12,073) has long since settled down into a picturesque community—i.e., looking just as it did when Hubert Humphrey first ran for Congress—its compact and charismatic business district filling a half dozen blocks along the south shore of lovely Lake Bemidji. With large mills still busily turning trees into wood products, Bemidji is a typically industrious lumber town, remarkable mainly for having assisted in the birth of that well-loved legendary duo of logging lore, Paul Bunyan and his blue ox, Babe (see sidebar *The Legends of Paul Bunyan*).

The main course of the GRR wraps around downtown Bemidji, so be sure to follow the Business Loop (old US-2), which passes up and over both the Mississippi River and Lake Bemidji while winding to downtown and a park where the town's big tourist draw, leviathan statues of **Paul Bunyan** and **Babe the Blue Ox,** have stood along the lakefront since their construction in 1937.

Along with Paul and Babe, Bemidji offers endless opportunities for water-skiing, canoeing, fishing, ice-fishing, and autumnal leaf-peeping (it's also the "Curling Capital of the USA"). Bemidji also has the northernmost outpost of a café destined to detain the most discerning road-food aficionado: the **Maid-Rite**

The Legends of Paul Bunyan

Like most other myths born on the American frontier, the legend of Paul Bunyan is obscured in the mists of time. The stories describing Paul's life—such as that when he was born it took five storks to deliver him and it took a whole herd of cows to keep him fed; that at just a week old he was big enough to wear his father's clothes; that he once bent a crowbar and used it as a safety pin to hold his pants together; that he was able to fell trees an acre at a time, and he used to whistle through a hollowed-out log—are impossible to trace, though their widespread popularity is due primarily to a public relations man at the Red River Lumber Company, William Laughead.

Beginning in 1914, and continuing for the next 20 years, Laughead and the lumber company, which was owned by the Walker family (founders of the Walker Art Center in Minneapolis), published a series of illustrated booklets recounting the stories already in general circulation around the logging camps. The booklets bore the full title *The Marvelous Exploits of Paul Bunyan as Told in the Camps of the White Pine Lumberman for Generations, During Which Time the Loggers Have Pioneered the Way through the North Woods from Maine to California, Collected from Various Sources and Embellished for Publication.*

The first large statue of Paul and Babe was built in 1937 in Bemidji, where they now stand along the lake. Statues of Paul and Babe were later built in nearby Brainerd, Minnesota, and others can be found in logging towns from coast to coast, like Klamath, California, and Bangor, Maine.

Walleye pike is a mild whitefish sought by Midwest anglers from May through the cold of February. The walleye found in Minnesota restaurants all come from Red Lake, site of the only commercial walleye fishing allowed by law.

Diner (218/444-7224), at 1602 Bemidji Avenue across from the lake near the information center. A classic diner, it's open from 7:30 AM for hearty meals and homemade rhubarb pies. For a nice lunch or dinner try **Union Station** (218/444-9261), in the old railroad building at 128 W. 1st Street, a bar and restaurant serving pastas, steaks, the ever-present walleye, and the best wild-rice salad around. For late-night dining, **Dave's Pizza** (218/751-3225) at 15th and Irvine is open till 11 PM (midnight on weekends).

Bemidji's many motels include the family-oriented **Hampton Inn** ($100; 218/751-3600 or 800/776-3343), situated on the lake at 1019 Paul Bunyan Drive, with its own beach and complimentary canoes available to guests. For more info, stop by the **visitors center** (800/458-2223), next to Paul and Babe on the lakeshore. Besides boasting a fireplace made with stones from every U.S. state (apart from Alaska and Hawaii, which weren't states when the fireplace was built), the visitors center shares space with a small **museum** ($1.25) of taxidermied wildlife and odd historical items—including Paul Bunyan's ax and oversized underwear.

Bemidji to Grand Rapids: The Big Fish

Leaving downtown Bemidji along the edge of the lake, the GRR makes a series of backcountry loops past tree farms and at least six of the state's 10,000 lakes, crossing US-2 twice before snaking into Grand Rapids 100 miles later. The road hugs red pine- and aspen-wooded shores and crosses the ever-widening Mississippi eight times, while numerous signs point to unseen resorts, which in Minnesota don't offer luxury so much as proximity to good fishing. Fishing is serious business hereabouts, as is evident from the frequency of signs advertising Leeches-Minnows-Nightcrawlers.

If you're just passing through, one place to set aside some time for is about halfway along, in the hamlet of Bena. Right along US-2, a 65-foot-long tiger muskie, with a 14-foot-wide

Big Fish Supper Club

mouth, welcomes customers to the popular **Big Fish Supper Club** (218/665-2333). As seen in that classic Chevy Chase road-trip movie *National Lampoon's Vacation,* the friendly café is open for three meals a day, except during the winter.

Grand Rapids

Navigational headwaters of the Mississippi River, **Grand Rapids** (pop. 7,764) is a small Frank Capra–esque kind of place, known for its four large in-town lakes (there are over 1,000 in this part of the state) and a great bridge over the river. The town—which is proud of its recent rating as the 47th Best Small Town in America—can be a bit confusing in its layout, but its compact size makes sightseeing manageable.

Grand Rapids is very proud of its most famous daughter, **Judy Garland,** and whoops it up every July with a festival in her honor.

The city sits along the western edge of the famed Mesabi Iron Range and includes viewing sites at a handful of **open pit mines.** The iron mines are a thing of the past, but Grand Rapids is still a major lumber town, and you can tour the impossible-to-miss **Blandin Paper Mill** (free; 218/327-6682). One of the world's largest paper producers, Blandin owns most of the surrounding forests and turns the trees into the stock onto which magazines like *Time* and *Sports Illustrated* are printed.

Three miles southwest of Grand Rapids, well signed along the Great River Road and equidistant via US-169 or US-2, the fine **Forest History Center** (daily in summer, weekends only rest of the year; $8; 218/327-4482) is a living-history replica of a 19th-century logging camp, complete with nature trails through the surrounding woods and energetic lumberjacks rolling logs and telling tall tales.

In the center of town, the **Itasca Heritage and Arts Center** ($4; 218/326-6431) is housed in a squat, three-story Victorian Romanesque-style grade-school building at the crossroads of US-2 and US-169. Here you'll find the county

Cass Lake was home to Ka-Be-Nah-Gwey-Wence, whose Anglicized name was John Smith, an Ojibwa who lived to be 129 years old. It is said he never slept in a bed. It may be unrelated, but the lake enjoys a reputation for having some of the most beautiful and serene camping in the state.

historical museum, with the usual "Main Street" of banks, stores, services, and pell-mell displays of farm equipment and logging gear.

Grand Rapids' real draw is the self-proclaimed **World's Largest Collection of Judy Garland Memorabilia,** she of ruby-slipper fame having been born Frances Ethel Gumm in Grand Rapids on June 10, 1922. Truly a cradle-to-grave biographical assembly, the collection displays everything from her first crib to photos of her early performances as part of the Gumm Sisters, a family vaudeville group, to a final shot of her tomb in Hartsdale, New York. There are posters from most of her movies, and a copy of her costume from *The Wizard of Oz* (although the ruby slippers were stolen some years ago). In front of the building is a miniature Yellow Brick Road dedicated by some of the surviving "munchkins" who worked on the picture.

West of Grand Rapids, near Cohasset, a low ridge divides this area of Minnesota and distributes the rivers and streams into three watersheds: south to the Gulf of Mexico, north to the Hudson Bay, and east to the Great Lakes.

All of the artifacts are on display, alongside the house where she was born, at the **Judy Garland Museum,** 2727 S. US-169 ($7; 218/327-9276).

Aitkin

South of Grand Rapids, the land rivals Kansas for flatness, yet the mix of farms and forest continues to lend visual interest to what could otherwise be achingly monotonous. The GRR alleviates boredom with its sinuous irregularity, the curves always hinting at the proximity of the Mississippi. For most of the way the river itself remains hidden, although regular signs for boat landings confirm its presence, and on occasion its broad channel and tree-lined banks roll into view.

For nearly 70 miles south of Grand Rapids you will have this rural road to yourself; then at the single stoplight in **Aitkin** (pop. 1,770), the GRR joins busy Hwy-210, at the edge of the mid-state lakes region. Aitkin is best known as the site of the annual **Fish House Parade,** in which ice fishermen show off their one-of-a-kind refuges from the winter cold; this unique event is held every year on the Friday following Thanksgiving. Year-round, Aitkin is a nice, all-American

Some of the best pies in the land of great pies can be had 20 miles north of Aitkin in the riverside town of Palisade (pop. 150), where the wonderful **Palisade Café** (218/845-2214) at 210 Main Street sells all sorts of fresh homemade pies.

town, with a still-in-use 1930s movie palace (The Rialto, on Minnesota Avenue), and the very good **Aitkin Bakery,** at 14 NW 2nd Street.

Crosby

Watch your compass needle for signs of deflection as you proceed to the small but tidy town of **Crosby,** the center of Minnesota's "forgotten" iron range, the Cuyuna. The flood-prone mines have died out, but the surrounding landscape still bears evidence of mining's heyday, with lakes and hills created by subsidence and strip mining, and also by contemporary gravel quarrying. Crosby itself has a nice park fronting onto Serpent Lake, complete with a brightly colored Chinese dragon, while **Croft Mine Historical Park** (daily in summer; tour $3.50; 218/546-5466), well posted on the edge of Crosby, profiles the iron-mining industry, covering immigration and labor issues as well as the actual mining process. Machinery, period buildings, a gift shop, and a simulated underground tour round out the site's features.

Between Grand Rapids and Brainerd, the official GRR takes a slow and somewhat scenic route along country lanes, though you'll save many hours (and not miss that much) by taking US-169 and Hwy-210.

South of Crosby, the GRR leaves the truck traffic and takes to the cornfields and sumac-laced forests again, passing as many barns as houses, the occasional lakeside hideaway, and some rural town halls; for a thumbnail overview of the area's settlement history, keep an eye peeled for the historical markers along the way.

Brainerd

At roughly the geographical center of the state, **Brainerd** (pop. 13,178) is a medium-sized Minnesota town that played a starring role in that offbeat Coen brothers movie, *Fargo*.

A huge Wausau paper mill along the banks of the river notwithstanding, the economy of this part of the state benefits greatly from recreation. In Minnesota this means lakes: over 400 within a 50-mile radius, with over 150 resorts or campgrounds on their shores. Brainerd, the commercial center of it all,

Cream of Wheat is one of the many cereals made in Minneapolis.

began life in 1871 when the Northern Pacific Railroad chose to cross the Mississippi River here. The rail yards are still in the heart of town beneath the giant water tower, which resembles a Las Vegas–style medieval castle. The historic downtown has been badly "malled" by outlying shopping plazas, but among the discount merchandisers, pawn shops, and empty storefronts there are still a few points of light, such as the **Front Street Cafe** (218/828-1102), at 616 Front Street, across the tracks from that faux piece of Camelot. With free seconds on soups, mile-high meringue on the pies, and unbelievably low prices—plus a collection of commemorative plates to which words cannot do justice—the Front Street Cafe sets a hip standard for square meals.

South of Little Falls, the GRR continues on its meandering way, but you can switch over to the uglier but much faster US-10 or I-94 freeways for the ride into the Twin Cities without missing anything significant.

West of the river, don't be put off by the unprepossessing location of the **West Side Cafe** (218/829-5561) at 801 W. Washington Street: The fact that it's in a gas station doesn't detract a whit from the fact that it serves some of the best pies for miles around, in a setting akin to an old Woolworth's lunch counter. From seasonal rhubarb to tangy cherry to unusual carrot, none is too sweet, and the superb flaky crusts are baked to a full golden brown.

East of downtown Brainerd, the Paul Bunyan statue seen in the Coen Brothers movie *Fargo* has moved to a new home at **Paul Bunyan Land** (daily in summer; 218/764-2524) at 17553 Hwy-18, part of the 35-acre kid-friendly rural-history theme park.

The Fourth of July in Brainerd is a big event, with marching bands, rock bands, and parades—plus a rubber duck race down the Mississippi River.

Many chain motels are clustered along the GRR (Hwy-371) and on Hwy-210 heading west out of Brainerd.

For a good overview of the region's recreational potential, stop by the Brainerd Lakes Area Chamber of Commerce's **Welcome Center** (800/450-2838), at 7393 Hwy-371, five miles south of Brainerd.

Crow Wing State Park and Little Falls

South of Brainerd, the GRR speeds along Hwy-371, which yearns to be an Interstate for the 30-odd straight miles it takes to reach Little Falls. Exceedingly flat and awash in a sea of corn, the region gives no hint of the Mississippi River except at **Crow Wing State Park** ($5; 218/825-3075). Native Americans, missionaries, fur-trappers, and lumberjacks made Crow Wing a thriving town until the 1870s, when the forced removal of the Indians and the shift of trade to the rail crossing at Brainerd turned Crow Wing into a ghost town. These days only cellar holes, a cemetery, and a single surviving home remain around the old townsite, while trails, a picnic area, and campsites spread out beside the confluence of the Mississippi and Crow Wing Rivers.

Across the Mississippi from Monticello, 2.5 miles downstream from Elk River off US-10, the **Oliver H. Kelley Farm** "living history" center preserves the place where the Patrons of Husbandry, an agricultural education and lobbying organization better known as The Grange, was founded in 1867.

Little Falls

At **Little Falls** the GRR neatly misses the fast-food and gas claptrap that has sprung up along the busy Hwy-371 bypass, proceeding instead through the heart of town, which would probably still be recognizable to aviator Charles Lindbergh, who spent his boyhood summers here a century ago. Running along the west bank of the river, the GRR passes by the **Charles A. Lindbergh House and History Center,** 1620 Lindbergh Drive S. (daily in summer, limited hours rest of the year; $7; 320/616-5421). The house, which sits a mile south of town on a beautiful

Charles Lindbergh

Twin Cities: Minneapolis and St. Paul

The Twin Cities share the Mississippi River but have little else in common. In general, Minneapolis has fashion, culture, and reflective glass, while St. Paul has a greater small-town feel, more enjoyable baseball, and the state capitol. Together, the Twin Cities are a typically sprawling American metropolis with an atypically wholesome reputation: safe, liberal-minded, welcoming to strangers, and inclined to go to bed early. Don't fret, there's enough to keep the visitor fully entertained.

The best place to stop and get a feel for the Twin Cities is at the **Minneapolis Sculpture Garden,** on Lyndale Avenue along I-94 (daily 6 AM–midnight; free). This is one of the city's finer urban oases, with over 40 works of art ranging from Henry Moore to Claes Oldenburg's Pop Art *Spoonbridge with Cherry.* Running over the I-94 freeway, a sculptural footbridge adorned with words from a John Ashbery poem connects the sculpture garden to Loring Park and the pedestrian greenway to downtown (an in-line skater's heaven). Next to the garden is the **Walker Art Center** (closed Mon.; $6; 612/375-7622), rightfully renowned as one of the nation's finest contemporary art museums and an architectural marvel.

Across the Mississippi in St. Paul, the **Minnesota History Center** (closed Mon.; $10; 651/259-3000), off I-94 at 345 W. Kellogg Boulevard, will further convince you there's more to Minnesota than meets the eye. Start with the Tales of the Territory historical exhibit on the third floor, to ground yourself in the mid-19th century setting in which the state of Minnesota rapidly emerged out of a thickly forested Indian territory. There's also a truly interactive Music in Minnesota section, where you can record your own version of the Twin Cities' disco smash, "Funkytown," or dance in a re-created 1940s swing ballroom. Exhausting? Maybe. Worth it? You bet!

Another advantage of visiting the Twin Cities: Baseball fans have a choice. As of 2010, the **Minnesota Twins** play outdoors at **Target Field,** on 3rd Avenue, between 5th and 7th Streets. The unaffiliated, independent, and generally anarchic **St. Paul Saints** play outdoors at usually sold-out **Midway Stadium,** 1771 Energy Park Drive, north of I-94 at the Snelling Avenue exit ($5–10; 651/644-3517). The fun-loving Saints fans cheer as freight trains rumble past the outfield fences.

Practicalities

The Twin Cities are on opposite sides of the Mississippi River, at the crossing of the I-35 and I-94 freeways. (It was a bridge along the I-35W freeway that collapsed in August 2007, killing 13 people; in typically cooperative Minnesota fashion, the replacement bridge was finished in just over a year.) Located seven miles south, the Minneapolis–St. Paul International Airport (MSP) is served by 10 major airlines, with Northwest Airlines exercising the home field advantage. Drivers here, like all Minnesotans, are friendly and helpful, and the city grids are easy enough to navigate by car, although on-street parking becomes more scarce as you approach the downtown areas. There are many parking garages (called "ramps"), and rates vary considerably.

Eating is perhaps the area where the Twin Cities really show off their multicultural vitality to best advantage. There are large Central American, Caribbean, Somali, Kurd, and Hmong populations here, and the traditional dominance of meaty northern and eastern European cuisine is being challenged by a bumper crop of new and different places to eat all over town. For a sample, head to **Chino Latino,** 2916 S. Hennepin Avenue (612/824-7878), where the "Sushi Loco" selections capture all the complexity and contradiction underlying the Twin Cities' calm surface. For a taste of old-style Minnesota, there's still **Nye's Polonaise Room** (612/379-2021), just over the bridge from downtown at 112 E. Hennepin Avenue, a dimly lit, plush-boothed, 1950s surf-and-turf restaurant with nightly sing-along Polka concerts. For another touch of the Twin Cities' past, nearby **Kramarczuk's Sausage,** 215 E. Hennepin Avenue (612/379-3018), has fat wursts and borscht, as well as *varenyky, nalesnyky,* and *holubets* (a.k.a. dumplings, crepes, and cabbage rolls), all served up cafeteria-style beneath coffered tin ceilings and the gaze of a giant Miss Liberty holding aloft her lamp.

continued on next page

Twin Cities:
Minneapolis and St. Paul
(continued)

Without doubt, the best road-food place is the decidedly un-gentrified, 24-hour **Mickey's Dining Car** (651/222-5633), right in downtown St. Paul at 36 7th Street, opposite the bus station. Haute cuisine it ain't, and half the regulars treat it as a social service agency, but this 1937 O'Mahony is a fine example of what has become an endangered species since the proliferation of double arches.

If you're traveling on an expense account, downtown Minneapolis has the hotel for you: the sleek, modern **Graves 601** ($250 and up; 800/543-4300), at 601 N. First Avenue. In St. Paul, the **St. Paul Hotel** ($200 and up; 651/292-9292 or 800/292-9292), at 350 Market Street, across from the beautiful Ordway Music Theatre, is a 1910 gem built for the city's rail and mill tycoons and has a rooftop gym. For a unique stay, try the **Covington Inn** ($140–200; 651/292-1411), a tugboat B&B moored on the Mississippi opposite downtown St. Paul. Otherwise, look to the Interstate beltways for the national chains, particularly I-494 between the airport and Bloomington's 100-acre **Mall of America,** the nation's largest.

The **Greater Minneapolis Convention and Visitors Association,** 40 South 7th Street (612/661-4700), can provide complete information on hotels, restaurants, and attractions.

stretch of the Mississippi, bears the unusual distinction of having been restored with the meticulous guidance of "Lucky Lindy" himself. Lindbergh wanted the site to honor his father, a five-term U.S. congressman, as well as himself, and so it does. Exhibits also illustrate the junior Lindbergh's life and achievements after his historic solo flight across the Atlantic in 1927. There is little mention of Lindy's public admiration for Adolf Hitler, but the museum does display Lindy's 1959 VW Beetle, which he drove over 170,000 miles on four continents.

The Burma-Vita Company, based just west of Minneapolis, began erecting advertising signs along Hwy-61 near Red Wing and Hwy-65 near Albert Lea back in 1925. Over the next 38 years, these signs and their witty rhymes appeared in nearly every state in the United States and made **Burma-Shave** one of the most recognized brand names in American business.

Driving the Twin Cities

South of Little Falls, agriculture continues to dominate the landscape, but as our route approaches the junction with I-94 at St. Cloud, the loss of farms foreshadows what is to come downriver. For nearly 100 miles, the GRR does its best to offer a scenic alternative, but sprouting subdivisions and suburban mini malls make it hard to enjoy. I-94 parallels the GRR and the Mississippi River all the way through the heart of the Twin Cities, and for better or worse it's pretty much the closest you'll get to a riverside highway. If you were hoping to follow the river through this stretch (by car, at least), you're out of luck.

WISCONSIN

Heading out of St. Paul along the industrialized Mississippi riverbanks, the GRR crosses the St. Croix River at Prescott, Wisconsin, and wends south on Hwy-35 across a portion of the glacial plain whose rolling hills, sown in corn, account for an important part of the nation's breadbasket. The fertile soil here, as throughout the Midwestern grain belt, is a product of drift: pulverized soil left by

On the Minnesota side of the Mississippi River, US-61 runs as a very fast and fairly scenic freeway, four lanes wide with near-continuous river views almost all the way south to La Crosse, Wisconsin. One place along here worth a linger is the town of **Wabasha,** as seen in the Walter Matthau/Jack Lemmon film *Grumpy Old Men.* Another is **Lake City,** where banners and billboards proclaim it the Birthplace of Water Skiing.

mile-thick ice sheets scouring the ancient sediments of an inland sea for about two million years. Farther south, however, the GRR enters a very different landscape, known as the **Driftless Region,** an area of limestone bluffs and rocky uplands bypassed by all that rototilling glaciation. Stretching south into Illinois, and covering an area four times the size of Connecticut, the Driftless Region affords dramatic views, wildlife habitat, and a setting for one of the more painful episodes in Native American history, the devastating Black Hawk War.

The GRR follows two-lane Hwy-35 from Prescott south for nearly 100 miles, staying within closer view of the Mississippi for longer stretches than almost anywhere else on the route.

Hwy-35: Main Street USA

At **Maiden Rock,** about 50 miles southeast of St. Paul, Hwy-35 enters the heart of the Driftless Region, picking its way between steep bluffs and the wide Mississippi. Small towns, populations numbering only in the hundreds, cling to the margin, competing for the distinction of having the longest Main Street in the nation, if not the world; for some of these long hamlets the GRR is nearly the *only* street. These towns wear their age well, too busy with fishing or loading up barges to make themselves pretty for tourists, or to tear down every old building that no longer seems useful. Most of these towns have at least a gas station, open late, and a roadhouse with Old Style or Pabst neon in the windows, open even later. Along with the riverside scenery, most also have a single tourist attraction: Amish crafts in **Stockholm,** a cheese factory in **Nelson,** and **Alma** has an observation platform and small café over Lock and Dam No. 4, where you

On an island near Red Wing, Minnesota, the **Prairie Island Nuclear Power Plant** is the northernmost of a half dozen uranium-powered generating stations located along the Mississippi.

can watch river traffic "lock through." In **Pepin,** midway between Maiden Rock and Alma (and roughly midway between Minneapolis and La Crosse), there's a replica of the log cabin where Laura Ingalls Wilder was born in 1867. Her first book, *Little House in the Big Woods,* was set here, though it's hard now to imagine that this was still the wild northwestern frontier back then (but it was).

Trempealeau

At the sleepy hamlet of **Trempealeau** (pop. 1,319), the GRR would have you zig-zag right through town, but detour a block down toward the river's edge to find the **Historic Trempealeau Hotel, Restaurant & Saloon** ($110 and up; 608/534-6898), sole survivor of an 1888 downtown fire—maybe that's why the whole joint is smoke-free. The hotel dining room offers a surprisingly eclectic menu, from steak and seafood to Tex-Mex and vegetarian dishes; just head for the neon sign reading Delicious Food. The rooms are nice (and cheap!), and the hotel also sponsors an excellent annual outdoor music series beginning with a Reggae Sunsplash the second weekend of May and featuring bands you've heard of throughout the summer (Steppenwolf and Asleep at the Wheel have appeared more than a few times). The hotel rents canoes and bicycles to hardy souls desiring to try either the **Long Lake Canoe Trail** or the 100-mile network of **paved bikeways** that passes through town.

Just south of Trempealeau, the GRR crosses US-53. Consider taking this Interstate-wannabe into La Crosse to avoid the uninteresting 12 miles of stop-and-go traffic through Holman and Onalaska, La Crosse's northern abutters.

La Crosse

La Crosse (pop. 51,818) was named by fur-traders who witnessed local Winnebago Indians playing the game. It's an attractive place, but you wouldn't know that coming into town from the north; thanks to the town's location astride the I-90 freeway, mile after mile of food-gas-lodging establishments compete for attention. Successfully run the gauntlet and

Between Minneapolis and La Crosse, Winona State University's **KQAL 89.5 FM** plays an excellent range of commercial-free pop, punk, and world beat music.

your reward will be finding the century-old downtown, the tidy residential neighborhoods, and the leafy University of Wisconsin—La Crosse campus. Slap *Spartacus* on the theater marquee and the whole place could easily be mistaken for a giant Eisenhower-era time capsule.

The biggest sight to see in La Crosse is the **World's Largest Six-Pack,** right on the GRR on the south side of downtown, at 1111 S. 3rd Street. La Crosse–based Heileman was widely recognized around the upper Midwest for its "Old Style" brand beer, and its brewery was famous for its giant fermentation tanks painted to look like the world's largest six-pack. Alas, a few years ago

Heileman's brewery was bought out by a multinational company, which immediately whitewashed over what had long been a cherished local landmark. Then a local company, City Brewing, took over operations and brought back the big Six Pack, which when full holds enough beer to fill seven *million* real-life six-packs.

World's Largest Six-Pack

The best overview of La Crosse is two miles east of downtown at the end of Main Street: **Grandad Bluff,** a lofty 590 feet over the city, gives a grand view of the Mississippi and the two states along its opposite shore. The view is a balm to any aesthete jangled by the commercial neon carpet that welcomes travelers, too, for La Crosse actually looks rather attractive from above. Listen closely and you might hear the University of Wisconsin marching band practicing below.

Six miles east of La Crosse, **West Salem** was the boyhood home of Pulitzer Prize–winning novelist Hamlin Garland, whose bittersweet stories of 1860s Wisconsin farm life have earned him a reputation as one of the finest American authors. His honest, social-realist books include the autobiographical *Son of the Middle Border* and an excellent collection of stories, *Main-Traveled Roads.*

La Crosse Practicalities

La Crosse food tends toward the hearty and all-American. For good ol' drive-in burgers, chili dogs, root beers, and milk shakes, nothing beats **Rudy's** (608/782-2200), northeast of downtown at 10th and La

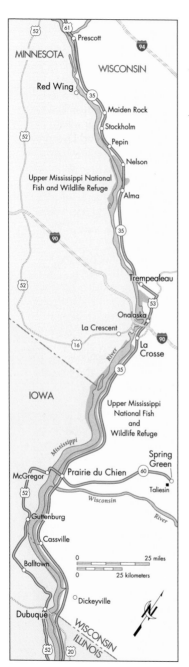

Crosse Streets, where roller-skating car-hops feed you 10 AM–10 PM daily, March–October. Rudy's sponsors "Cruise Nite" every Tuesday, June–September.

The Pearl, a polished-to-perfection confectionery at 207 Pearl Street (608/782-6655), offers such indulgences as fluorescent Blue Moon ice cream while the Andrews Sisters harmonize in the background. More grown-up pleasures, in the shape of nearly 400 bottled beers (plus a dozen microbrews on draught), WiFi, and popcorn await you at the awesome **Bodega Brew Pub,** right downtown at 122 S. 4th Street (608/782-0677). Travelers seeking something wholesome, fresh, and filling should head to the deli of the **People's Food Co-op,** at 315 S. 5th Avenue, between Cass and King (608/784-5798).

For accommodations, look to I-90 for the national chains, while local motels line Hwy-35/US-61 (the GRR, sometimes a.k.a. Mormon Coulee Road.) Just south of downtown, the **Guest House Motel,** 810 South 4th Street ($55; 608/784-8840) offers British hospitality, comfortable clean rooms, a café, and outdoor swimming pool.

For more detailed information, call the La Crosse Area Convention and Visitors

Black Hawk War

One name recurs frequently as you travel along the northern Mississippi River: Black Hawk was the leader of the Sauk and Mesquakie Indians of northern Illinois during the feverish era of American expansion into the newly opened Louisiana Purchase in the late 1820s. Indian fighters were held in high esteem by 19th-century Americans; consider that a number of U.S. Army officers sent against Black Hawk later became president, including William Henry Harrison, Zachary Taylor, Abraham Lincoln, Jefferson Davis, and Andrew Jackson. After Jackson rode his Indian-fighter reputation into the White House, Black Hawk and his people were forced to leave their rich Illinois cornfields as settlers and lead miners moved in.

In 1832, as newspapers around the United States demanded the extermination of any and all Indians, Black Hawk (who was around 65 years old at the time) moved back to Illinois to regain the tribe's lost lands along the Rock River. In response, President Jackson sent in the army, and as Black Hawk and his 300 or so supporters tried to withdraw back across the Mississippi, soldiers and frontier militias attacked them at what became known as the **Battle of Bad Axe,** near the present town of Victory, midway between La Crosse and Prairie du Chien. When Black Hawk and his men came forward under a white flag, an Army gunboat opened fire, while many of the Indian women and children who had succeeded in riding log rafts across the river were slaughtered on the other side. By various accounts, some 150 of Black Hawk's people were killed. Black Hawk himself was soon captured and imprisoned, then paraded around the United States in chains. After he died, his skeleton was displayed in the governor's mansion in Iowa, like a trophy.

Bureau (608/782-2366 or 800/658-9424) or visit its **information center** in leafy green Riverside Park, where a 25-ton, 25-foot-tall statue of Hiawatha greets river traffic with arms crossed and a politically incorrect plaque reading: Me Welcome You to Visitor Center.

Spring Green

Frank Lloyd Wright's famous country house and studio, Taliesin (tally-ESS-en), is in **Spring Green,** 70 miles east of Prairie du Chien via Hwy-60. Fully guided tours of the architect's private residence and architecture school he inspired are offered daily May–October; ticket prices vary, depending on what's included in the tour ($17–80; 608/588-7900). Spring Green is also home to the state's biggest tourist trap, the incredible **House on the Rock** (daily; $30; 608/935-3639) with its "World's Largest" merry-go-round, kitschy collections of everything from dolls to replicas of the Crown Jewels, and the eponymous house, standing atop a 450-foot-high rock.

Hwy-35

For most of the nearly 60 miles between La Crosse and Prairie du Chien, the GRR (Hwy-35) is again confined to the margin between the tall gray and yellow bluffs and the impressively wide, lake-like Mississippi. At times the roadway is so narrow that the few houses have to climb three stories up the irregular wooded slopes, while the railroad tracks on your right are suspended over the water on viaducts. About halfway along, there's a maze of small islands around the mouth of the Bad Ax River, with the occasional blue heron poised like a Giacometti sculpture in algae-covered sloughs. Dotting the curves alongside the road are a series of historical markers old enough to be artifacts themselves; most are related to the tragic **Black Hawk War** of 1832.

Midway along this scenic stretch of highway, 34 miles north of Prairie du Chien between the riverside hamlets of De Soto and Genoa, the **Great River Roadhouse** (608/648-2045) at 1006 Hwy-35 is a great place to stop and stretch your legs— and your stomach, feasting on the roast chickens, good pizza, tangy barbecue, and cold beers.

Prairie du Chien

Named by early 19th-century French voyageurs, **Prairie du Chien** (duh-SHEEN) could be re-christened Prairie du

South of Prairie du Chien, across from McGregor, Iowa, is the spot where **Louis Joliet** and his Jesuit companion **Jacques Marquette,** after coming down the Wisconsin River in 1673 while searching for a route to the Orient, caught their first sight of what became known as the Mississippi River.

Kwik-Stop or Prairie du Pabst by the modern traveler cruising along the GRR on downtown's West Blackhawk Avenue. The town's main attraction is the posh **Villa Louis** (daily May–Oct.; $9; 608/326-2721), which embodies the wealth that could be made in the fur trade back when every European dandy's head sported beaver-pelt hats. Built by the state's first millionaire, the house boasts one of the finest collections of domestic Victoriana in the country; signs point you here from all over town.

IOWA

In its 140-mile course across Iowa, the GRR passes swiftly but unmistakably across the cultural and geographic North-South Divide. Separated by the Mississippi River from the rough topography of Wisconsin's Driftless Region, the southeastern corner of Iowa offers instead a taste of the state's trademark rolling plains covered with corn and soybeans. Menus are different, too: Cattle here are raised for meat instead of milk, and Iowa is a leading producer of hogs (one of the state lottery games is called Bring Home the Bacon, while radio ads encourage you to "Eat more pork—the other white meat"). So say goodbye to walleye and hello to barbecue.

Running along the western bank of the Mississippi, our route tends to the tops of the bluffs, too, rather than to their base, which means the river is often spied from a distance and seems unrelated to the rolling landscape; fortunately it continues to guide the curves of the road. Other than Dubuque, our route passes through towns so far from the beaten path they don't even rate a fast-food strip or Wal-Mart—appreciate this while it lasts.

Marquette: Effigy Mounds National Monument

Immediately across, and effectively underneath, the long

bridges over the Mississippi from Prairie du Chien, **Marquette** is a homey, workaday community that verges on quaint—so long as you manage to turn a blind eye to the garish pink elephant advertising its Isle of Capri Riverboat Casino complex. Unless you're a gambler, the main reason to visit is three miles north of Marquette, right along the riverbank: the **Effigy Mounds National Monument** ($5 per car; 563/873-3491), which preserves 2,500 acres of natural riverside ecosystems plus more than 200 distinct burial mounds, many shaped like birds and animals. The unusual mounds are traces of the native people who lived along the Mississippi from around 500 BC to the time of first European contact; for more on these fascinating if little-known prehistoric Americans, see *The Mound Builders* sidebar. The visitors center has exhibits on the archaeology of the mounds, and a dozen miles of hiking trails reach from the river to restored vestiges of the native tallgrass prairie.

Forty-six miles west of McGregor is the Bohemian (as in Czechoslovakia, not bearded poets) town of **Spillville,** where **Antonin Dvorak** completed his symphony *From the New World* in 1893. The Main Street house (319/562-3569) where he stayed now leads a double life: Displays on Dvorak are upstairs, while downstairs is an incredible show of wooden clocks carved by the Bily brothers, depicting everything from the Twelve Apostles to Charles Lindbergh.

McGregor

Just south of Marquette, near the foot of the "original" Pike's Peak—Zebulon Pike came up the Mississippi before he went out west to Colorado—**McGregor** (pop. 871) is a river town whose enticing old saloons and storefronts are a fine reason to stop and stretch your legs, watching the boat and barge traffic or simply wandering along the water. The slogan of McGregor's tourism promotion effort is "Intriguing Stores on Historic Shores," and for once the copywriter prose is about right. A number of browsable an-

McGregor was the hometown of the five children who grew up to found the **Ringling Brothers circus.**

tique-and-collectible shops line the GRR through the four-block main business district, and McGregor also boasts about the only riverside hotel on the entire Great River Road: the family-friendly **Holiday Shores Motel** ($50–80; 563/873-3449) at the foot of Main Street.

The Mound Builders

The broad area between the Mississippi River and the Appalachian crest is rich in early American history, but the human story here goes back way beyond Daniel Boone and Abraham Lincoln to an era not often discussed in textbooks. From around 800 bc until ad 1500, this region was home to two successive prehistoric cultures which were roughly simultaneous with the legendary Mayans and Aztecs of Mexico, but are now all but forgotten, remembered solely for the massive earthen mounds they left behind.

The older of these two prehistoric peoples is known as the Hopewell culture, since the first scientific studies were conducted in 1891 at a farm owned by a man named Hopewell. Some 50 years earlier, the mounds had already become famous, as stories spread tracing their construction back to a "lost race" of mysterious origin, not unlike the Anasazi of the desert Southwest. As the Hopewell culture began to decline, around ad 500, another culture, called the Mississippian, came into being. Similarities between these two hunter-gatherer cultures, with their far-flung trading networks and hierarchical societies, are much greater than their differences, but archaeologists consider them to be completely distinct from one another. A key difference: Almost all of the Hopewell mounds

Just south of town, the 500-foot-high limestone bluff known as Pike's Peak is one of the highest points anywhere along the Mississippi River and has been protected at the center of spacious green **Pike's Peak State Park** (563/873-2341), with hiking trails, scenic viewpoints, and a campground with a small store, hot showers, and RV hookups.

Guttenberg

Atop the bluffs, tidy frame farmhouses dot the landscape, with white barns, silos, and farmland aroma accompanying US-18 and US-52 as they loop inland south toward **Guttenberg** (pop. 1,987), another postcard-pretty old river town whose downtown lines the Mississippi. In fact, it's one of the few Mississippi riverfronts where the river itself is not hidden away behind levees, and a long green riverside park, just a quick two blocks east of

were rounded or conical, and built as burial sites, while Mississippian sites tended to be more rectilinear, with the mounds serving not as interments but as bases for long-vanished wooden structures built atop them. In Hopewell sites, buried along with the usually cremated human remains, archaeologists and treasure hunters have recovered a compelling array of artifacts—obsidian tools (from the Pacific Northwest), shell beads (from the Gulf of Mexico), and silver and copper objects (from the Great Lakes)—which give some hint of the quality of ancient Native American life.

Ohio is particularly well provided with these enigmatic earthworks; at the Hopewell Culture National Historic Park near Chillicothe, over two dozen burial mounds have been preserved by the National Park Service. West of Chillicothe, the low-lying Serpent Mound stretches for a quarter mile along a river, and over 100 other sites have been identified across the state.

Farther west on US-50, along the Mississippi at Cahokia Mounds State Historic Site (see page 57), the remnants of the largest prehistoric city in North America now sit across the river from St. Louis. North along the river, the Effigy Mounds National Monument in Iowa across from Prairie du Chien (see page 29) preserves yet more burial mounds, while down south, the Natchez Trace Parkway features the prehistoric Emerald Mound (see page 87).

the main highway, makes the downtown area a particularly pleasant place to stroll.

Guttenberg is indeed named in honor of Johannes Gutenberg, 15th-century inventor of printing from moveable type. Local legend has it that an official of French descent purposely added the extra "t" after German residents won a vote to change the town's name from the original Prairie la Porte. Germanic surnames still predominate in the local phone book, and the two main streets, which run perpendicular to the Mississippi, are named Schiller and Goethe.

On the north side of town, the GRR takes an up-close look at the prairie's geological underpinnings as it cuts down to the river's edge. From the downtown area, it's a quick walk upriver to the concrete

Different towns along the Iowa stretch of the GRR act as the finish line for the trans-Iowa **RAGBRAI**, a 500-mile, weeklong mass bike ride that sees 10,000 cyclists cruising across the state every July.

walls of Lock and Dam No. 10. Besides giving a sense of the massive engineering that attempts to tame the Mississippi, the locks are also home to an aquarium that offers a quick biology lesson through displays of live specimens of many of the river's fish and invertebrate species.

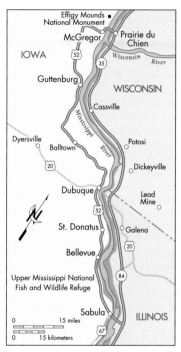

There are great views to be had in the first few miles of Iowa's GRR route south of Guttenberg. About 10 well-signed miles south of Guttenberg, you can take the Cassville ferry across the Mississippi from Millville and visit the unique Dickeyville Grottoes, or stay on the Iowa side and cruise through the Germanic eye-blink towns that dot the rolling uplands between Guttenberg and Dubuque. Midway along, tiny **Balltown** in particular is worth a stop to sample the food and decor at **Breitbach's,** 563 Balltown Road (563/552-2220), a bar and restaurant that's so old President Millard Fillmore issued the permit allowing it to open.

Dickeyville Grottoes

Across the river from Dubuque, the Wisconsin town of Dickeyville is home to one of the most interesting folk-art environments along the Mississippi: the **Dickeyville Grottoes** ($1 suggested donation; 608/568-3119). Started by Father Mathias Wernerus in 1920 as a memorial to three local boys killed in World War I, and worked on as a community project by his followers up through the 1960s, the

Dickeyville Grotto

Dickeyville Grottoes consist of a series of caves, alcoves, and shrines made of poured concrete almost completely covered in shells, shards, minerals, and costume jewelry. Along with the expected Catholic religious themes, parts of the Grottoes also exhibit a unique vein of patriotic Americana—highlighted by the "Patriotism in Stone" memorial to Christopher Columbus, George Washington, and Abraham Lincoln. Maintained as a public park, with almost no commercialization, the Grottoes are open 24 hours every day at 305 W. Main Street, adjacent to the Holy Ghost Catholic Church, a block west of US-61.

Dickeyville can be reached a number of ways. It's a quick shot north along US-151 from Dubuque, or from Prarie du Chien you can follow scenic Hwy-133 along the east bank of the Mississippi. If it's summertime and you want an up-close look at the Mississippi, make your way to Cassville, a historic frontier town that holds one of the river's few surviving car ferries. The ferry has been running since the 1840s and now runs Wednesday through Sunday in summer, weekends only in May and October ($12 per car; 608/725-5180).

Dubuque

At the southern end of a very enjoyable ride, cruising up and down sculpted hills and winding past miles of Iowa prairie and river towns, the GRR rolls into **Dubuque** (pop. 57,686), named for the 18th-century French voyageur Julien Dubuque, who unsuccessfully mined lead on land acquired from the Spanish. Finding lead wasn't the problem—Indians had dug lead by hand as early as 1680 for trade with the English—but getting it to market was. After the steamboat's invention and forced removal of native tribes in the late 1820s, mineral wealth became a major catalyst to settlement of the tri-state area around Dubuque, as town names like Potosi, Mineral Point, New Diggings, and Lead Mine attest. During the Civil War, just five counties around here supplied all the lead for the entire Union war effort.

On the inland side of the compact downtown, a grand view of the city and the Mississippi valley can be had from the top of the **Fenelon Place Elevator,** a historic funicular cable car that proudly holds the title of "world's steepest, shortest scenic railway" ($1; daily April–Nov. only). Still hauled up and down the hill by a 15-hp motor in the head house, the elevator is a mini version of those in Pittsburgh and the Swiss Alps. Hop on at the east end of 4th Street and ride up to the plush residential district on the hilltop.

On the other side of downtown, the Dubuque waterfront has been recharged by the **National Mississippi River Museum,** 350 E. 3rd Street (daily; $11; 563/557-9545), one of the two biggest and best museums dedicated to the history and culture of Old Muddy (the other one is on River Island in Memphis). A large collection of historic riverboats is highlighted by the steamboat *William M. Black,* an official National Landmark, while other galleries include a National Rivers Hall of Fame that tells the stories of explorers and adventurers like Lewis and Clark and John Wesley Powell. The introductory film, *River of Dreams,* is narrated by Mr. Lake Wobegon himself, Garrison Keillor.

The museum complex is at the heart of the America's River complex, which also has the inevitable casino plus docks for scenic sightseeing and gambling boats, a nice riverside promenade, a café in the restored train depot, and the **Grand Harbor Resort** ($99 and up; 563/690-4000), a deluxe hotel and 25,000-square-foot water park.

Dubuque is a very meat-and-potatoes place when it comes to food, and as in most of the Midwest, you should plan to dine early to catch restaurants before they close. Near the Fenelon Place Elevator, the **Shot Tower Inn** at 290 Locust Street (563/556-1061) is a very popular pizza place with an upstairs deck and beer by the pitcher. The one standout in Dubuque is the **Pepper Sprout,** 378 Main Street (563/556-2167), where the range of dishes (and the big-city prices) proves that "Midwest Fine Dining" is not an oxymoron.

East and west of Dubuque, US-20 offers a pair of excellent detours off the Great River Road. The ball field created for the movie *Field of Dreams* has become a minor tourist mecca for rural **Dyersville,** 30 miles due west of Dubuque via US-20 or the surprisingly scenic, gravel-paved Heritage Trail, which runs along an old railroad route.

South of Dubuque, the GRR follows US-52 back up the bluffs past Julien Dubuque's original lead workings and across 45 miles of upland farms and wooded bottoms until the next Mississippi crossing at Sabula.

Galena

If ever there's a place where you can truly step back in time, **Galena** (pop. 3,647) is it: Pass through the floodgates that protect the town from the namesake river (and the US-20 highway), and it's like entering Brigadoon. Spawned by Wisconsin's mid-19th-century lead-mining rush, Galena became the social and cultural capital of the Upper Mississippi basin. In the 1840s, while Chicago was still a mean collection of tents in a swamp around Fort Dearborn, and the Twin Cities were but a trading post in the woods around Fort Snelling, Galena was producing upwards of 75 percent of the world's lead, and the town was filled with bankers, merchants, and speculators who built mansions, hotels, and emporiums stuffed with fine goods and furnishings from around the world. This part of the Driftless Region saw some of the greatest wealth and commerce of the upper Mississippi, with Galena alone higher in population—some 15,000 lived here during the Civil War—than the entire Minnesota Territory.

But the California gold rush, played-out lead mines, a river silting up from miner-induced erosion, and a national economic panic all drove Galena to become a handsome ghost town that nobody bothered to tear down. For 100 years it slumbered, but beginning in the 1960s Galena was resurrected as a quaint tourist town. The brick warehouses were converted into shops and galleries, and anything but the most subtle, hand-carved signage was banned: In Galena, preserving the historical complexion of the streetscape isn't just a good idea, it's the law. The outskirts, especially along the US-20 frontage, are fairly typical roadside sprawl, and there are still a few everyday businesses in the historic core (including a funeral parlor and a large and busy metal foundry), but the overall feel is of a long-ago era. Even the innumerable galleries and shops selling T-shirts and "collectibles"

Northwestern Illinois was the site of many skirmishes between settlers and Indians during the **Black Hawk War** of the early 1830s.

The hilly **Driftless Area** is so-called because the landscape here was never smoothed out by Ice Age glaciers.

Mrs. Grant didn't like the fact that her late husband's statue in Galena's **Grant Park** showed the general with his hand in his pocket. Not that she wanted it changed. "Oh, no!" she told the sculptor, "Leave it as it is, but dear me, I've told that man 20 times a day to take his hand out of his pocket."

Commander of the Union Army and President of the United States.
1822 – 1885

can't spoil the remarkable effect of the place. One essential: Park the car and *stroll*.

Besides the integrity of its mid-19th century buildings, Galena is famous as the town that saw a local store clerk win both the Civil War and the presidency. The modest **Ulysses S. Grant Home** (daily 9 AM–5 PM except major holidays; $2 donation; 815/777-0248) sits up Bouthillier Street in a quiet residential neighborhood across the river from downtown. Given to the general by a grateful group of local Republicans, the house is now a state historic site restored to the period immediately preceding Grant's move to the White House. A small museum behind the house traces Grant's life, from the Civil War to the presidency to his burial in Grant's Tomb.

Galena Practicalities

Even if you're blind to Galena's manifold aesthetic and historical delights, you'll probably enjoy its wide variety of food and lodging options—the clearest proof of the town's popularity with tourists. The downside of this is that most of the long-standing local cafés have given way to knickknack boutiques and fancy bistros. Unless you're staying at a B&B, the place to get a good breakfast is a half mile west of downtown along US-20, at **Emmy Lou's** (815/777-4732). There is, fortunately, still one great old downtown place for a good, fairly cheap, and always cheerful dinner: the **Log Cabin** (815/777-0393), at 201 N. Main Street. Galena's oldest restaurant, with a great big green-and-red sign that predates the town's anti-neon ordinance, the Log Cabin is also known as "The House of Plenty" and has been serving up a mix of industrial-strength Greco-Italian food, steaks, and seafood since 1935. Galena also has a pair of great pizza places: **Cannova's** at 247 Main Street (815/777-3735) and **Procento's,** a block away at 105 Franklin Street (815/777-1640).

There are some 60-odd hotels, guest homes, and historic inns here in "the B&B capital of the Midwest." The central **DeSoto House** ($150 and up; 815/777-0090), at 230 S. Main Street, was U. S. Grant's headquarters during his 1868 presidential campaign; the entire place was tastefully modernized during a recent $8 million renovation. Smaller and perhaps more relaxing, the friendly **Farmer's Guest House,** 334 Spring Street ($125 and up; 815/777-3456), is also right downtown. If you're just passing through, the cheapest decent sleep in town is at the **Grant Hills Motel** (around $65; 815/777-2116) east of town at 9372 E. US-20.

The Galena/Jo Daviess County Convention and Visitors Bureau operates an excellent **visitors center** (815/777-0203 or 800/747-9377), across the river via a pedestrian-only bridge, in the old Illinois Central Railroad depot at the base of Bouthillier Street. Stacks of brochures cover everything from accommodations to bike tours. This is also the best place to park the car, as spaces are at a premium in the often-crowded downtown area.

St. Donatus

Fifteen undulating agricultural miles south of Dubuque, the tiny hamlet of **St. Donatus** is widely advertised as a historic and picturesque Luxembourg village, mainly thanks to the handsome masonry of the **Gehlen House** (563/773-8200), a 150-year-old home now used as a restaurant and B&B. Other eye-catching structures are the Catholic church and **Pieta Chapel** atop the adjacent Calvary Hill; if you wish to make a pilgrimage up the Way of the Cross, start behind the church burial ground, east of the Kalmes General Store. There's a nice view from the top—the other set of spires across the valley belongs to the German Lutheran St. John's Church.

From the end of November to the beginning of March, the **American bald eagle** nests along the middle and upper Mississippi. The best place to catch sight of one is below any of the dams, where turbulence keeps the river from icing over and fish injured or stunned by the dams make easy prey for the great bird.

Bellevue and Sabula

The GRR (US-52) returns to the Mississippi valley at **Bellevue,** with its lengthy Main Street and Riverfront Park beside Lock and Dam No. 12. Bellevue earns its name when you sit on the porch of the restored **Mont Rest B&B** ($150 and up; 563/872-4220), at 300 Spring Street, and take in the sweeping 270-degree panorama over the Mississippi.

Continuing south, the GRR stays in sparsely populated wooded lowlands through **Sabula,** an island of a town created by the Corps of Engineers when the pool above Lock and Dam No. 13, 16 miles downstream, flooded out the surrounding plains. Sabula takes its name from the Latin sabulum (sand). The river here is nearly four miles wide. Sabula's encompassing levees provide fine wetlands bird-watching, especially for bald eagles.

ILLINOIS, IOWA, AND MISSOURI

The Great River Road route along the middle Mississippi starts in northwestern Illinois, at the southern edge of the Driftless Region, and proceeds through sandy floodplain and fertile prairie, nipping back and forth across the ever-locked and dammed Mississippi between Illinois, southern Iowa, and the generally more-developed Missouri uplands. Here, small towns bypassed by much of the 20th century are more likely to be forlorn than quaint, a prelude to those southern states in which local ordinances appear to require the public display of rusty appliances. With a few exceptions—such as the historic Mormon town of **Nauvoo** or Mark Twain's hometown of **Hannibal**—our route now mostly runs through communities whose best years may have passed. This stretch of the GRR also includes one of the most dramatic sections of the entire route: the 25 miles around **Grafton, Illinois,** at the northern doorstep of **St. Louis.**

South of St. Louis, I-55 is the recommended route, as it bypasses a long string of auto dealerships, appliance stores, shopping centers, and other prefab conveniences lining old US-61. Passing by the enticing old river town of **Sainte Genevieve,** the GRR crosses the Mississippi once again, ambling back to the corn, soybeans, and cicadas of Southern Illinois. Accents, "Bar-B-Q" signs, and Baptist churches leave no doubt that our route has entered the South; in summer the heat and humidity confirm this with a vengeance. Fortunately, after leaving the "American Bottom" the GRR skirts the edge of the **Shawnee National Forest,** whose shade brings up to 25°F of relief from

the temperatures along the roadside fields on a sunny July day. Occasional levees, raised roadbeds, and brackish seasonal ponds are reminders that the mile-wide Mississippi is only temporarily out of sight of the GRR, which finally cross-

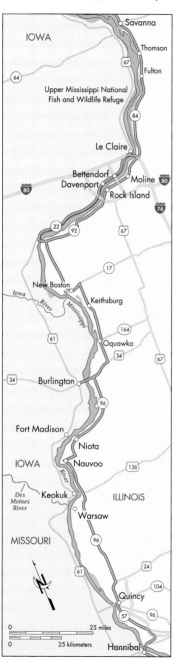

es into Kentucky beside the giant turbid confluence of the Mississippi and Ohio Rivers at Cairo.

Savanna: Mississippi Palisades

Across the Mississippi from Iowa, **Savanna,** Illinois, is an old railroad town that has grown into an antiques center, offering three antique mini malls along the main drag. Savanna maintains a few pretty Victorian mansions up on the heights, but for a truly attractive vista take a detour north along Hwy-84 from the end of the Iowa bridge to the 2,500-acre **Mississippi Palisades State Park** (815/273-2731), with its great eroded bluffs (popular with rock climbers), 13 miles of hiking trails (brilliant fall color in the forested ravines), and fine river views. There's camping, too, with hot showers and RV hookups.

Between Savanna and the I-80 beltway around the Quad Cities are nearly 50 flat miles of river valley, dotted with small historic river and railroad towns mixed in with new commercial and residential construction. Agriculture is conspicuous, too, and the sandy soils between Savanna and Thomson are particularly known for their melon crops. While the Mississippi for the most part

Thomson, 20 miles south of Savanna on Hwy-84, is the self-proclaimed Watermelon Capital of the World and celebrates its **Melon Days festival** every Labor Day weekend. Country music, carnival rides, watermelon-eating contests, and free watermelon are the traditional highlights.

stays invisible from the GRR, the industry on its banks is clearly evident, especially at night. River access is at hand via a handful of recreation areas in the Upper Mississippi National Fish and Wildlife Refuge.

Le Claire, Iowa

On the northeastern edge of the Quad Cities, just off the I-80 freeway, lies the little town of **Le Claire** (pop. 2,734), famous once for its river pilots but now best remembered as William F. "Buffalo Bill" Cody's home. The **Buffalo Bill Museum** (daily in summer, weekends only the rest of the year; $2; 563/289-5580), on the waterfront at 200 N. River Drive, is dedicated to Cody's life. LeClaire is also home to the **Faithful Pilot** (563/289-4156), at 117 N. Cody Road on Le Claire's main street (US-67), One of the best restaurants in the entire Quad Cities region, the Faithful Pilot has creative, high-quality cuisine, a good wine list, fine microbrews, and a small bar at the back with views over the river.

The Quad Cities

Straddling the Mississippi at its confluence with the Rock River, the **Quad Cities**—Moline and Rock Island, Illinois, and Davenport and Bettendorf, Iowa—encompass an enormous sprawl of some 400,000 residents. While much of the cityscape is dominated by heavy industry, particularly on the Iowa side, points of interest are sprinkled throughout.

Along the river at the heart of the Quad Cities, adjacent to downtown Rock Island, is the former namesake of that city, now called Arsenal Island for the U.S. Army facility based there. Despite the look of the gatehouse at the southern entrance, the island is open to the public; besides an arsenal museum and Civil War cemeteries, there's a very good **Corps of Engineers visitors center** (daily; free) on the island right next to Lock and Dam No. 15, where the operation of the locks can be seen from a penny-pitch away.

The first railroad bridge over the

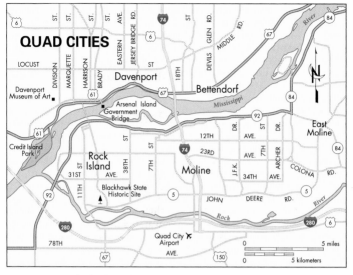

Mississippi linked Rock Island and Davenport in 1856. The railroad was promptly sued by a steamboat company whose craft was mortally attracted to the bridge piers. The plaintiffs argued that bridges violated their navigation rights; the defense lawyer's elegantly simple—and successful—rebuttal was that a person has as much right to cross a river as to travel upon it. That lawyer was Abraham Lincoln. Today the railroad crosses the river on the upper deck of the old iron Government Bridge, which swings open for the tows entering the locks; cars crossing between Rock Island and Davenport can ride the humming lower deck or take the modern concrete highway span below the dam.

The **Davenport Museum of Art** (closed Mon.; 563/326-7804), at 1737 W. 12th Street, has a good regional collection featuring Thomas Hart Benton and Grant Wood, along with parodies of Wood's most famous painting, *American Gothic.* Davenport is also home to the **River Music Experience,** 131 W. 2nd Street (closed Sun.; free; 877/326-1333), an interactive museum exploring the many different sorts of music that have grown up along the Mississippi River. Frequent, free live concerts are held on the plaza outside.

Davenport celebrates

the music legacy of native son and cornetist Leon Beiderbecke with the annual **Bix Beiderbecke Memorial Jazz Festival,** held at the end of July. A statue of Bix stands along the river, next to wonderful old (circa-1930) John O'Donnell Stadium, where the minor-league **Quad Cities River Bandits** (tickets $7; 563/324-3000) play their home games.

coronetist Leon Beiderbecke

Quad Cities Practicalities

In downtown Davenport, the only large Mississippi River city not cut off from Ol' Muddy by a flood wall, look to the historic downtown area around the River Music Experience, where you'll find several eateries and cafés. Away from downtown Davenport, off I-80 exit 292, the original **Iowa Machine Shed Restaurant,** 7250 Northwest Boulevard (563/391-2427), draws families from near and far for its huge portions of roast pork and other Midwest faves (like the famously good pies).

In Downtown Moline, a half dozen blocks along 5th Avenue between I-74 and 14th Street hold everything from the French-infused Vietnamese fare of **Le Mekong** at 1606 5th Avenue (309/797-3709), to the extraordinary **Lagomarcino's,** 1422 5th Avenue (309/764-1814), a candy store and soda fountain that still uses those conical paper cups in solid metal holders and serves drinks like phosphates in a setting virtually unchanged since it opened in 1908. Order a strawberry shake here and the flavor will come from scoops of real strawberries ladled over freshly made vanilla ice cream.

Rock Island's old downtown, 2nd Avenue, has experienced something of a revival with the appearance of a riverboat casino a block away; one pleasant result is "the District," centered on the 2nd Avenue pedestrian mall. One great place hereabouts is the **Blue Cat Brew Pub,** along the riverside at 113 18th Street (309/788-8247), where salads, seafood, and desserts go way beyond your average

MAID RITE
THE ORIGINAL
HAMBURGS

pub fare, and the beers range
from traditional lagers and
ales to more esoteric concoc-
tions (orange coriander *Hefe
weis,* anyone?).

For a truly regional diner
experience, make your way
to a **Maid-Rite Diner;**
there's one in Moline at 2036
16th Street (309/764-1196). A strictly upper-
Midwest phenomenon whose faded logo, "Since 1926," can
often be seen on old brick buildings or historic commercial
storefronts as far away as Minnesota, the local Maid-Rites are
unusually bright and polished, and they come heartily
recommended.

Illinois: the Yellow Banks

Zig-zagging for nearly
100 miles south of the
Quad Cities, the GRR
picks its way along a series
of back roads through
Illinois floodplain and prairie, where frequent small
farming towns serve as reminders of the need for frequent stops by early stages,
steamboats, and railroads.
Most of the towns seem not to

steamer *G.W. Hill* landing at Burlington, Iowa,
c. 1900

have changed much since the last steamboat or train whistle
blew, although now there's neon in the bars, vinyl and alumi-
num siding on the houses, and farmers with high-powered four-
by-fours on the roads.

Nearly 45 miles south of the Quad Cities beltway, the
GRR passes tiny **New Boston,** at the mouth of the Iowa
River. The town is a historical footnote these days, having
been surveyed by the young Abraham Lincoln after his
stint in the army—a tour of duty during which his only
combat was against mosquitoes, he later recalled. Along the
river farther south, near **Keithsburg,** a sign welcomes travelers to **Yellow Bank country,** named for the deep layer of
sand exposed in the river valley in this region. Because of
this deposit, visitors can find sandburs and even cactus in

the Big River State Forest south of town. Keithsburg used to be one of a number of button manufacturing centers located along the middle Mississippi: Freshwater clams were dredged from the river bottom and their shells were used for making pearl buttons.

Burlington and Niota

Across the Mississippi River via an austere modern suspension bridge, **Burlington** was the frontier capital of Iowa, founded in 1808 and holding many Victorian homes and commercial buildings. Awarded "Great American Main Street" status from the National Trust for Historic Preservation in 2004, Burlington also has a riverboat casino, a great **Maid-Rite diner** (112 W. Division Street), and very busy downtown rail yards—one-time home base of the Burlington Northern Santa Fe (BNSF) railroad conglomerate.

At **Niota,** the ghost of a town that marks the next crossing south of Burlington, a nifty old 1920s double-decker swing bridge (trains below, cars on top) crosses the Mississippi, landing on the west bank next to a huge old state prison at the historic town of Fort Madison, Iowa.

Nauvoo

Founded in 1839 by the Church of Jesus Christ of Latter-day Saints (LDS), the town of **Nauvoo**—a Hebrew-sounding word its founding father was told meant "the beautiful location"—was named by Mormon leader Joseph Smith, 12 years after he received the Book of Mormon from the Angel Moroni. Smith and many of his followers had spent the previous winter jailed in Liberty, Missouri, and by 1846 they were effectively exiled to Utah, but for a few years Nauvoo was among the largest settlements on the western frontier, with hundreds of log cabins and brick buildings and a population of some 6,000 Mormon believers. After 150 years of relative peace and quiet, in the 1990s the Mormon church started a massive, $30-million program of historic preservation, turning Nauvoo into a top destination for Mormon pilgrims and retirees. The "restoration" of Mormon Nauvoo, and the influx of well-heeled Mormon immigrants, has been on such a big scale that many non-Mormons have felt under siege. Visitors to Nauvoo will certainly

In **Oquawka, Illinois,** 10 miles northeast of Burlington, Iowa, a roadside marker points out the spot where in 1971 a circus elephant (named **Norma Jean Elephant!**) was killed by lightning.

Mormons in Illinois

If you're passing through Nauvoo, you'll have plenty of opportunities to learn about Mormon history and religion. Nauvoo is a mecca for Mormons, or "Latter-day Saints" (LDS), as church members prefer to call themselves. In 1839, a dozen years after receiving their new gospel via the Angel Moroni, the Mormons purchased a large tract of swampy land along the Mississippi River, then set about draining swamps and building a city. Within a few years, Nauvoo was not only the largest LDS settlement in America, but the 10th-largest city in the United States. The emergence of such a powerful little theocracy (with its own well-armed militia) generated resentment among outnumbered neighbors, and even some internal dissent. The friction escalated to violence on both sides, finally culminating in the 1844 arrest of Joseph Smith Jr., church founder and president, for having sanctioned the destruction of printing presses used by some church members to question his leadership. While in the nearby Carthage jail, Smith was lynched by a mob and so became one of the Mormons' first martyrs. Amid ensuing disputes over church succession and renewed hostilities with non-Mormon neighbors, most residents followed Brigham Young across the Mississippi on the famous exodus to Salt Lake City.

Given Smith's martyrdom, the fact that he's buried here, and the Brigham Young migration's roots in the town, it's little wonder that Nauvoo attracts Mormon pilgrims by the busload. The Utah-based LDS have sponsored a massive restoration of old Nauvoo buildings, and the town now ranks as one of the capitals of historic preservation in the United States. Most of old Nauvoo is operated essentially as a big museum, totally free and open to the non-LDS public.

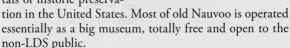

have plenty of opportunities to learn about Mormon history and religion, but for the moment at least the part-preserved, part-restored townscape has a broad interest as a mostly non-commercialized reminder of what frontier America looked like in the years before the Wild West was finally "won."

The biggest change in Nauvoo has been the reconstruction of the original Mormon **temple,** which, from the time it was finished in 1846 until it was burned down in 1848, was the largest building west of Philadelphia. An exact replica of the original, the new temple took more than three years to complete and was dedicated in 2002. The temple, located at 50 Wells Street, has a remarkable series of stone capitals carved with sunburst motifs, and a 165-foot-high steeple capped by a statue of the Angel Moroni. Other interesting Mormon-related sites include the store run by Joseph Smith and the home of Brigham Young. The home and workshop of John Browning, inventor of the repeating rifle, has been restored along Main Street, south of the present downtown area. There's also a massive **outdoor pageant** (8 PM Tues.–Sat.; free; 800/453-3860) every July, celebrating the early, pre-Utah years of the LDS community.

Nauvoo Practicalities

For a map of the town and visitor information, stop by the huge **LDS Visitors Center** (daily; free; 888/453-6434), at the north end of Main Street. The town operates its own info center, too: the **Nauvoo Chamber of Commerce** (217/453-6648), at 1295 Mulholland Street, opposite the historic Hotel Nauvoo.

The annual **Nauvoo Grape Festival,** held each Labor Day weekend at Nauvoo State Park south of town, celebrates the wine business that arose after European immigrants moved onto farms abandoned by the Mormon exodus. Nauvoo also developed a blue-cheese industry in the 1920s, after Prohibition shut down the winemaking trade. The centerpiece of the festival is a combination custom car show and the "Wedding of the Wine and Cheese," a medieval-style pageant borrowed from Roquefort, France.

Restaurants and lodgings are clustered along Mulholland Street (Hwy-96, a.k.a. the GRR) within the few blocks of downtown Nauvoo. For picnic supplies, try the **Nauvoo Mill and Bakery** (217/453-6734) at 1530 Mulholland Street near the Shell station. For fried chicken, cold beers, or a Friday night fish fry, try the **Draft House** (217/453-6752) at 1360

Mulholland Street. The circa-1840s **Hotel Nauvoo** (217/453-2211), at 1290 Mulholland Street, is particularly well regarded for its belt-straining buffets and is also the town's most characterful place to stay (rooms run $65–125).

Warsaw

For a scenic dozen miles south of Nauvoo, the GRR returns after long absence to the banks of the Mississippi, shaded by native hickory and oak, and then sidesteps yet another opportunity to enter Iowa, this time via US-136 west to Keokuk. Staying on the east bank, the GRR follows a series of farm roads past gravel pits and fields for most of the 40-mile run down to Quincy.

Warsaw lends its name to a variety of geode found locally in profusion; inside, **Warsaw geodes** grow calcite crystals. Across the Mississippi, **Keokuk geodes** grow quartzite crystals inside their stony spheres.

First stop south of Nauvoo is **Warsaw,** where the photogenic old downtown is kept alive by a pair of very welcoming stops: **J. Doggs Bar and Grill,** 605 Main Street (217/256-4088), is locally famous for juicy pork tenderloins, and the **Warsaw Brewery,** on the riverfront at 900 N. 6th Street (217/256-4393), which opened in the 1860s, closed in the 1970s, and was resurrected in 2006 as a fine place for a cold beer. At the south end of town the GRR threatens to turn amphibious as it rolls down past a towering grain elevator to the Mississippi's edge, bends south along the base of the bluffs past old house trailers, scruffy fields full of wildlife—including wild turkeys and river turtles waddling along the roadside—and old kilns visible in the limestone. The road passes, finally, back into Illinois's signature cornfields, planted in the fertile floodplain of the Mississippi.

Quincy

Midway between the Quad Cities and St. Louis, **Quincy** (pop. 40,366) is a modest-sized city, Germanic enough in its heritage to consider Pizza Hut an ethnic restaurant. A bastion of abolitionists before the Civil War, Quincy was also home to anti-abolitionist Stephen Douglas, the incumbent Illinois senator whose campaign debates with Abraham Lincoln put that tall country lawyer on the path to the White House.

The GRR follows the riverfront and again the pilot's wheel is missing, but the giant span of the Bayview bridge over the Mississippi will leave no doubt as to which way to turn to stay

Drop the top on your convertible and maybe you can land yourself a travel companion during the **World Free Fall,** an annual skydiving event that fills Quincy's skies with thousands of jumpers from all over the planet. Held at Baldwin Field between the first two weekends in August, the Free Fall is the legacy of one Thomas Baldwin, whose pioneering parachute jump from a balloon into a Quincy park in 1887 earned him two world exhibition tours.

on track. However, most of the city perches on the tall bluffs above the GRR and is worth a drive-through, if only to sample its textbook variety of residential architecture. Check out the **Gardner Museum of Architecture and Design** (Wed.–Sat. 1–5 PM; $3; 217/224-6873), in the old public library downtown on Maine and 4th, for an overview of both those topics. Then take a walk or drive through the East End, an area roughly bounded by Maine and State Streets between 16th and 24th. Filled with historic mansions along quiet tree-canopied streets, it's the perfect place to practice distinguishing your Queen Anne from Tudor, and your Prairie Style from Gothic Revival.

If you have thus far avoided the tried-and-true cooking of the **Maid-Rite** chain, Quincy gives you a chance to fix this oversight: There's one at 507 N. 12th Street (217/222-7527).

If you plan to spend the night, you'll find the national chains downtown out on Broadway near I-172. If you prefer antiques to HBO in your room, try the **Kaufmann House** ($45–65; 217/223-2502), in the heart of the historic mansions at 1641 Hampshire Street.

For more information, call or drop by the tourist information center in the **Villa Kathrine** (800/978-4748), that hard-to-miss, turn-of-the-20th-century Moorish residence on the bluffs overlooking the Mississippi, just south of the US-24 bridge.

Hannibal

It doesn't take a literature professor to figure out who **Hannibal's** most famous resident was: His name prefaces half the signs in town, and the names of his characters preface the other half. Cross the Mississippi River on the I-72 Mark Twain Memorial Bridge, shop at the Huck Finn Mall or swim at Mark Twain Lake, then spend the night at Injun Joe's Campground or the Tom N' Huck Motel. Turn onto 3rd Street (the Great River Road) near the Hotel Clemens and park yourself in the heart of historic old Hannibal, and visit the Mark Twain Home and Mark Twain Museum. Take a very expensive ride on the almost miniature *Mark Twain* riverboat, docked at the Center Street Landing; browse through books by and about Twain at the Becky Thatcher Bookshop; or eat Mark Twain Fried Chicken at the Mark Twain Dinette. Not to detract from the credit due him, but don't look for any subtlety or modesty surrounding Mark Twain's achievements here.

Most of this Twainery is located downtown, within a few blocks of the Mississippi River, and enjoyment requires at least a passing familiarity with (and fondness for) *Tom Sawyer,* Twain's fictionalized memoir of his boyhood here. A statue of Tom and Huck stands at the foot of Cardiff Hill, and two blocks south, the white picket fence featured in that book still stands in front of the **Mark Twain Boyhood Home** (daily; $9; 573/221-9010), at 208 Hill Street,

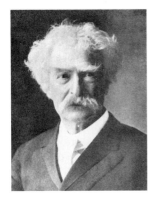

The Twain mania is so overwhelming that little is made of Hannibal's other famous sons. Baseball lovers searching for some mention of **Joseph Jefferson "Shoeless Joe" Jackson** will look in vain; there is none. Neither is there much mention of **Bill Lear,** inventor of the car radio, the 8-Track tape, and the Lear jet, who was born here in 1902.

where young Samuel Clemens (Twain's real name) grew up in the 1840s. The historic site preserves a half dozen buildings, including his father's law offices and the drugstore above which the Clemens family also lived. The home of Tom Sawyer's "girl next door," Becky Thatcher, is actually across the street, and the upstairs parlor and bedrooms have been re-created to evoke the era. The main **Mark Twain Museum** recently moved into a much larger space in an ornate Victorian building two blocks away at 415 N. Main Street but is still part of the same operation. Exhibits, including a steamboat pilot's wheel and numerous first editions, bring to life scenes from Twain's Mississippi novels.

A pair of high hills bookend Hannibal (pop. 17,757), and climbing up either (or both) gives a grand overview of the town and the broad Mississippi, its historic lifeblood. On the north side, climb up the staircase from the Tom and Huck statue to the top of Cardiff Hill, where the **Mark Twain Memorial Lighthouse,** built in 1935 to celebrate the centenary of Twain's birth, offers a fine view. South of town, **Lover's Leap** is higher and more breathtaking—best visited by car or bike. Farther south of downtown along the GRR (Hwy-79) is Hannibal's most kid-friendly attraction: the **Mark Twain Cave** (daily; $15), where costumed guides spin tales about Tom and Huck on an hour-long tour.

Hannibal Practicalities

To immerse yourself fully in the Mark Twain experience, try the Mark Twain memorial chicken (or a Mississippi Mud milk shake) served all day at the **Mark Twain Dinette** (573/221-5300), at 400 N. 3rd Street, adjacent to the Mark Twain Home in what looks suspiciously like a converted A&W. A step up the culinary scale, **Ole Planters Restaurant** (573/221-4410) at 316 Main Street has a full range of lunches and dinners; dessert fans will want to sample the German chocolate pie, a specialty of the house. This species, like rhubarb, is predominantly found in pie cases along the middle Mississippi, so if you're planning a scientific sampling, start now. Away from downtown, the **Riverview Cafe** (573/221-8221), in the kitschy Sawyer's Landing along Hwy-79 south of Hannibal, has possibly the best kitchen in town, with a view that may indeed be worth the higher prices.

Consistent with its status as an international tourist attraction, Hannibal has plenty of motels, B&Bs, and campgrounds. The **Best Western** ($75 and up; 573/248-1150), at 401 N. 3rd Street, sits downtown at the foot of the old US-36 bridge. The national chains line up along busy US-61 west of downtown.

For a complete list of lodgings, restaurants, events, and tourist traps, pick up a free guide from the Hannibal **visitors center** (573/221-2477 or toll-free 1-TOM-AND-HUCK), at 505 N. 3rd Street. The most popular annual festival is **Tom Sawyer Days,** held the weekend nearest to the 4th of July, when children take part in the National Fence Painting Championship (a whitewashing homage to *Tom Sawyer*), a frog-jumping competition (remembering Twain's Gold Rush–era short story, *The Celebrated Jumping Frog of Calaveras County*), and the very messy Mississippi Mud Volleyball Championships.

Twain was a bit of an impractical investor, losing lots of money on lots of harebrained schemes while missing at least one spectacular opportunity, the telephone. Or so hindsight teaches us—but how much would you invest in a new invention by a guy who flies tetrahedral kites and makes devices to detect metal in the body? Twain said no, so **Alexander Graham Bell** took his invention to **J. P. Morgan** instead.

Louisiana and Clarksville

For the first 20-odd miles south from Hannibal, the GRR ascends and descends the densely wooded tops of bluffs, pausing at scenic turnouts for views across the Mississippi Valley, here many miles wide. In October, the upland forests are blazing with fall color that compares with any outside New England, and if you roll down the windows or stop to stretch your legs

If you've been keeping track, you'll have noticed the lock and dam numbering skipped No. 23 between Hannibal and Clarksville. There are 29 Army Corps of Engineers–operated **locks and dams** on the Mississippi, from the unnumbered ones in the Twin Cities to No. 27 at St. Louis.

during the summer, listen for the omnipresent buzz of cicadas in the tangled undergrowth.

Another icon of the lower Mississippi, one that has extended its range north, like the cicadas (and the fire ant), is the huge and pungent chemical plant on the south side of the town of **Louisiana** (pop. 3,863); ironically, considering current concerns about energy supplies, this plant was originally constructed by U.S. Army in the 1940s, to create synthetic alternatives to fossil fuels. The town itself, like a Hannibal without Mark Twain, has one of the Midwest's most intact Victorian-era streetscapes, full of 125-year-old brick cottages and warehouses, but looking like it has just about lost the battle against extinction.

A short ways farther south, **Clarksville** (pop. 480) is another GRR town with more of a past than a future, but some optimistic restorers of the riverfront historic block are counting on tourism to improve the town fortunes.

Claiming preeminence as the highest point along this stretch of the Mississippi River, 600-foot **Pinnacle Peak** is also noteworthy for the rusty remains of its old "Sky Ride" chair lift, which once carried riders over the GRR all the way to the top. Clarksville also boasts what may be the largest concentration of **bald eagles** in the lower 48 states; in winter months they feed by the hundreds below Lock and Dam No. 24, on the northern edge of town.

Winfield Ferry

Swinging away from the river south of Clarksville, the GRR reenters the corn belt in great straight stretches of road, rising and falling over rolling prairie still hilly enough that you can play peek-a-boo with approaching traffic over the miles of ups and downs, passing towns that often comprise little more than a few houses around a gas station and a grain elevator on a rarely used railroad siding.

At the hamlet of **Winfield,** 100 yards north of the only stop sign on this stretch of the GRR, there's a clearly visible sign for the **ferry** (daily year-round; $6; 618/396-2535), which crosses the Mississippi about three miles east of town, just below Lock and Dam No. 25, and shuttles across to Calhoun

County, Illinois. There are no fixed departure times: The operator leaves when all the customers waiting are aboard, or when the ferry is full, and returns when there's a fare to bring back or when he or she spots you waiting—so drive right up to where you can be seen, and if it's after dark, keep your lights on.

If the ferry isn't running, St. Louis's suburban edge is 20 miles south along Hwy-79.

Calhoun County

Wedged between the Mississippi and Illinois Rivers, the rural peninsula of **Calhoun County** is one of the best-kept secrets in the state of Illinois. Cut off from the rest of the "Land of Lincoln" and connected to neighboring Missouri by ferry only, Calhoun County is a world of its own. A third of the state's substantial peach crop is grown here on farms that have changed hands only a few times, if at all, since they were given out as land grants to veterans of the War of 1812; bypassing the summer farm stands, especially when the baseball-sized, plum-sweet tomatoes are in season, borders on criminal. A lucky few St. Louisians have weekend getaways here, too, alongside shacks and trailers that seem to accumulate debris like the Corps' dams accumulate Mississippi mud.

From the end of the Winfield ferry access road, detour south to the town of **Brussels** (pop. 150), whose public phone booth is possibly the town's sole civic improvement since the Coolidge administration, a handful of cafés and bars is evidence of its popularity with weekenders from St. Louis. The most popular haunt in Brussels is the venerable **Wittmond Hotel** (618/883-2345) across from the water tower and post office at the heart of Brussels. The dining room here serves delicious, all-you-can-eat, family-style meals (very popular on Sunday). It no longer rents rooms, but there's still a timeless bar and an even more ancient-looking general store—complete with dusty old merchandise that looks like it dates back to when the enterprise opened in 1847.

Getting to and around Calhoun County is a bit of an adventure. The main access is from the southeast, across the Illinois

River via the state-run, round-the-clock Brussels Ferry; there's also a bridge at Hardin 14 miles upstream. From the northern St. Louis area, the privately operated *Golden Eagle* (618/883-2217) runs across the Mississippi River from a landing outside St. Charles to **Golden Eagle,** Illinois. Last but not least is the ferry across the Mississippi from Winfield. Most of the ferries cease operation in the winter, but during summer they run more or less from dawn to midnight, sell local maps, and can offer basic visitor information. Road signs in Calhoun County are almost nonexistent, but just driving (or cycling!) around, getting lost and found, and lost and found again, is by far the best way to get a feel for this preserved-in-amber island in time.

The Illinois River and Père Marquette State Park

At the south end of Calhoun County, the Brussels Ferry takes all of two or three minutes to cross the narrow Illinois River, along which Marquette and Joliet returned to Canada after their failure to find a westward-flowing river to the rich lands of Cathay and the Far East. René-Robert Cavelier, Sieur de La Salle, came down the Illinois eight years later in 1681, on the first expedition to specifically target the Mississippi. It was La Salle who claimed the Mississippi territory for his sponsor, King Louis XIV of France, and who went all the way down to the Gulf of Mexico (Marquette and Joliet turned back after the confluence of the Arkansas River).

While the Mississippi may be muddy and less than pristine, at least one man is working to clean it up: Chad Pregracke spends his days hauling old tires, sunken refrigerators, and other light industrial discards out of the water. You can follow the progress at www.livinglandsandwaters.org.

If you're equipped for some hiking or biking, **Père Marquette State Park** is a short, well-signed, and definitely worthwhile three-mile detour upstream from the Brussels Ferry landing. The handsome **park lodge,** built by the Civilian Conservation Corps in the late 1930s, is noted for its 700-ton stone fireplace, massive tree-trunk roof supports, decorative ironwork, and outsized chess set in front of the ox-sized hearth that definitely can create a congenial chalet atmosphere, particularly if you time your arrival for evenings, midweek, or off-season to avoid the crowds. Cabins and lodge rooms are available for reasonable rates (from $99 for two; 618/786-2331). Expect holiday and fall foliage weekends to be booked up a year in advance; camping and tent rentals are also available (618/786-3323).

Following an old railroad route for much of the way, the 20-mile **Sam Vadalabene Bike Trail** between Père Marquette State Park and Alton is unquestionably the best venue for appreciating the scenery, even for a short walk, for Hwy-100 is a fast, divided highway whose drivers don't appreciate slowpokes.

Grafton and Elsah

North of St. Louis on the Illinois side of the Mississippi, the high-speed section of the GRR between Grafton and Alton is widely considered one of its most scenic stretches. Towering limestone bluffs, their curving faces pocked with caves  and overhangs, push the road to the edge of the broad lake formed by Lock and Dam No. 26. Before or after the drive, stop at the south edge of Grafton, where **Elsah's Landing Restaurant** (closed Mon.; 618/786-7687), at 420 E. Main Street, has something of a monopoly on good food in these parts; its made-from-scratch ethic pays off in all departments.

Speeding along Hwy-100 south of Grafton, it's easy to miss the turnoff for **Elsah,** but even if you have to turn around and come back, it's worth it to check out this tiny hamlet tucked away in a cleft in the palisades. Light years away from St. Louis, but only a half hour's drive away, Elsah is listed in the National Register of Historic Places in its entirety and is an architectural gem, with 19th-century cut-stone and clapboard buildings and narrow lanes reminiscent of some idyllic English country village. Two small B&Bs and the **Green Tree Inn** ($125; 618/374-2821) offer unexpectedly romantic getaways, a taste of New England here in southern Illinois.

Atop the bluffs over Elsah is the very Tudor campus of **Principia College.** A Christian Science institution of higher education, the campus and many buildings were designed by Art-and-Crafts master architect Bernard Maybeck.

South of Elsah, before the bluffs give way to grain elevators at Alton, you'll catch a glimpse of the **Piasa Bird** (PIE-a-saw) high on the wall of an old roadside quarry. Marquette and other early explorers mention a pair of huge pictographs on the cliff face, representations of the Illini Indians' legendary "bird that devours men." Faded by the 1840s, the original site was destroyed by quarrying. The current 20- by 40-foot replica, based on various eyewitness descriptions, resembles something from the notebook of an adolescent Dungeons and Dragons fan.

Alton

At **Alton,** 20 miles northeast of St. Louis, the riverfront turns decidedly urban. The GRR races along the water, past busy tugboat docks, sulfurous chemical plants, and towering concrete grain elevators, all along a great protective levee under a thicket of high-tension power lines. The main attraction here is the vivid green-and-orange (and hugely lucrative) *Argosy Alton* casino boat, formerly the *Alton Belle,* the first in Illinois when riverboat gambling was made legal in 1991.

In May 2005, an Alton fisherman pulled a **125-pound blue catfish** out of the Mississippi River, a world-record catch.

A life-sized statue of Robert Pershing Wadlow, the world's tallest human, stands on the campus of the **Southern Illinois University Dental School,** on College Avenue (Hwy-140) a mile or so east of the river. The Alton-born "gentle giant," who enrolled here in what was then a Baptist seminary in 1938, was 8 feet 11¾ inches when he died in 1940, at the age of 22.

Inland from the waterfront, however, Alton is surprisingly peaceful and quiet, its redbrick streets lined by mature trees and a range of modest but well-maintained 19th-century houses. Near 5th and Monument Streets at the south end of town, high on a hill above the riverfront, Alton's cemetery is dominated by a large column topped by a winged figure—a monument to one of Alton's most important individuals, the abolitionist newspaper editor Elijah Lovejoy. Widely considered to be the nation's first martyr to freedom of the press and freedom of speech, Lovejoy, a newspaper publisher and preacher, was lynched in Alton in 1837 by a mob of pro-slavery Missourians.

Six miles south of Alton, near the village of Hartford, keep an eye out for the signs to the **Lewis & Clark Historical Site,** a reconstruction of the winter campsite of the Corps of Discovery in 1803–1804. Recently expanded with a large state-run museum (closed Mon. and Tues.; free; 618/251-5811), the site sits opposite the confluence of the Missouri and Mississippi Rivers, which roll together in a muddy tide between swampy wooded banks.

The GRR Across St. Louis

The Great River Road has many routes in, around, and

across St. Louis, and they're all so poorly marked that you're sure to get lost trying to follow any of them. From Alton, US-67 crosses just below Lock and Dam No. 26, taking first the Clark Bridge (over the Mississippi) and then the Lewis Bridge (over the Missouri River). No prizes for guessing what *those* names refer to, since you enter the city on Lewis and Clark Boulevard (Hwy-367).

A good main, non-freeway route across St. Louis is Kings Highway, which runs north–south past many of the city's main destinations, including Forest Park and the Missouri Botanical Garden, before ending up at Gravois Avenue, part of old Route 66. From here, numerous roads give direct access to I-55 and US-61, both of which link up with the scenic GRR route south to Sainte Genevieve.

Where the Great River Road hops onto the I-55 freeway for its final approach into St. Louis, a road clearly marked GRR Spur leads to **Cahokia Mounds,** the remains of the largest prehistoric American city north of Mexico.

Collinsville: Cahokia Mounds

Old Route 66 followed today's I-270 around the north side of St. Louis, crossing the Mississippi River on the recently restored Chain of Rocks Bridge, but one of southern Illinois's biggest attractions sits directly east of the

Get a feel for St. Louis listening habits by tuning in to commercial-free **KDHX 88.1 FM.**

George Rogers Clark's fame as a war hero, Indian fighter, and explorer put him at the top of Thomas Jefferson's short list for leading an expedition into what became the Louisiana Purchase, but the aging Clark nominated his younger brother instead. Thus did **William Clark** join **Meriwether Lewis** for their historic journey to the Pacific.

Cahokia Mounds sit in the middle of the American Bottom, a floodplain whose gunpowder-black alluvial soils have long been considered among the richest and most productive in the world—for example, about 80 percent of the world's horseradish supply comes from right here, making the region the official **Horseradish Capital of the World.** However, Charles Dickens called it an "ill-favored Black Hollow" after enduring its mud, which had "no variety but in depth."

St. Louis

Founded by French fur trappers in 1764, St. Louis served for most of its first century as a prosperous outpost of "civilization" at the frontier of the Wild West. It was the starting point for the explorations of Lewis and Clark, and much later Charles Lindbergh, whose *Spirit of St. Louis* carried him across the Atlantic. Unfortunately, like many other American cities, St. Louis has suffered from years of decline and neglect; the population, which peaked at over 850,000 in 1950, is now less than half that, and the sale of the city's iconic beer, Budweiser, to the Belgian company InBev didn't exactly thrill many locals. Although it has all the cultural and institutional trappings of a major city, not to mention the landmark Gateway Arch, St. Louis is at heart a city of small neighborhoods, such as bluesy Soulard south of downtown, the Italian-American "Hill" (boyhood home of Yogi Berra), and the collegiate West End district near verdant Forest Park.

One thing you have to see when in St. Louis (you literally cannot miss it) is the **Gateway Arch** (daily; 314/655-1700), on the riverfront at the foot of Market Street. Rising up from the west bank of the Mississippi River, Eero Saarinen's stunning 630-foot stainless steel monument still dominates the city skyline, despite the disrespectful rise of nearby office towers. Under the legs of the Arch, which is officially called the

Jefferson National Expansion Memorial, the free and fascinating **Museum of Westward Expansion** chronicles the human wave that swept America's frontier west to the Pacific. A small elevator-like tram ($10) carries visitors up the arch to an observation chamber at the very top.

West of downtown around the Washington University campus, in Forest Park's 1,300 beautifully landscaped acres, museums of fine art, history, and science fill buildings that date back to the 1904 World's Fair, St. Louis's world-class swan song.

The **St. Louis Cardinals** (314/421-2400), one of the country's most popular baseball teams, play at retro-modern Busch Stadium, right downtown with views of the river and Gateway Arch. Games are broadcast on **KTRS 550 AM.**

Practicalities

Freeways and high-speed arteries reminiscent of Los Angeles make a car handy for navigating the St. Louis area—unless you have oodles of money for cab fares—and thanks to the city's sad history of replacing its landmark buildings with blacktop, you'll find plenty of parking lots around downtown.

For food, The Hill neighborhood is hard to beat: **Gian-Tony's** (314/772-4893), at 5356 Daggettt Avenue, is perhaps the best of a dozen classic neighborhood Italian places. Wherever you go, try the toasted ravioli, a local treat. Near Washington University, another great place is the slightly kitschy **Blueberry Hill** (314/727-4444), at 6504 Delmar Boulevard, a retro-1950s diner that has an excellent jukebox, very good burgers, and enough real-life credibility to sometimes attract the

continued on next page

St. Louis (continued)

likes of St. Louis–born father of rock 'n' roll, Chuck Berry, to play impromptu gigs.

No one leaves St. Louis without cruising old Route 66 southwest from downtown to **Ted Drewe's,** 6726 Chippewa Avenue (314/481-2652), a local institution famous for its many flavors of "concrete"—a delicious frozen dairy-and-egg-custard concoction so thick you can turn it upside down and not spill a drop. Nearby, fried chicken fans flock to **Hodak's,** 2100 Gravois Road (314/776-7292). One last Route 66 place has been going strong for more than 100 years: the **Eat-Rite Diner,** 622 Chouteau Avenue (314/621-9621), a plain blue-and-white cube serving up breakfasts and burgers 24 hours a day (Mon.–Fri.). As the sign says: "Eat Rite, or Don't Eat at All."

St. Louis doesn't have that much of a tourist trade (the muggy weather here in summer keeps most sensible people far away), so places to stay are relatively cheap. **Hampton Inn at Gateway Arch** ($99 and up; 314/621-7900) at 333 Washington Avenue, and the larger **Adam's Mark** ($125 and up; 314/241-7400) at 112 N. 4th Street, are two of the more popular downtown hotels. Away from the Arch, at the **Hyatt Regency at Union Station,** 1820 Market Street ($150 and up; 314/231-1234 or 800/233-1234), the opulently restored lobby, formerly the great rail center's vaulted waiting room, is worth seeing even if you aren't a guest. In another historic reincarnation, a quartet of stately old warehouses has been converted to house the **Westin St. Louis** ($150 and up; 314/621-2000), near the Arch, the river, and the baseball stadium at 811 Spruce Street.

The **St. Louis Convention & Visitors Commission** (314/241-1764 or 800/916-0092) operates a well-stocked information center downtown at 308 Washington Avenue, near the river and I-70.

Gateway Arch, off the I-55/70 freeway at exit 6. Clearly visible to the south side of the Interstate, the enigmatic humps of **Cahokia Mounds State Historic Site** are the remains of the largest prehistoric Indian city north of Mexico. Over 100 earthen mounds of various sizes were built here by the indigenous Mississippian culture while Europe was in the Dark Ages; the largest covers 14 acres—more ground than the Great Pyramid of Cheops. But don't expect the works of the pharaohs: Symmetrical, grass-covered hills sitting in flat, lightly wooded bottomlands are what you'll find here. The view of the Gateway Arch in distant St. Louis from the 100-foot-top of Monks' Mound lends an odd sense of grandeur to the site, and a sophisticated Interpretive Center (hours vary; 618/346-5160) is a recommended first stop for its exhibits, award-winning multimedia orientation show, and guided and self-guiding tours.

The nearest town to the Cahokia Mounds is **Collinsville,** a pleasant little place that's nearly-world-famous for its 170-foot-high **World's Largest Catsup Bottle,** which rises high above 800 S. Morrison Avenue (Hwy-159), a quarter mile south of Main Street, on the grounds of what used to be the Brooks Catsup Company. This decorated water tower was constructed in 1949 and restored by the people of Collinsville in 1993; it has since been adopted by Collinsville as a super-size symbol of local pride and perseverance.

Not quite on the same scale as the mounds or the catsup bottle, the nearby Route 66 town of Mitchell holds the landmark, 85-year-old **Luna Café,** north of the I-270 freeway along old Route 66 at 201 East Chain of Rocks Road (618/931-3152).

Sainte Genevieve

South of St. Louis, to avoid the sprawling suburbia, take I-55 as far as exit 162, where you can rejoin the GRR by picking up US-61 south. If you don't blink, you may even catch sight of one of Missouri's rare pilot's-wheel signs as the busy road ascends a ridge with a fine western panorama. About 55 miles south of St. Louis's I-270/255 beltway, the GRR reaches the outskirts of **Sainte Genevieve,** one of several French trading posts established along the Mississippi in the wake of La Salle's 17th-century expedition. The town's new trade is tourism, as the antique shops and upscale restaurants clearly illustrate, but the beauty of Sainte Genevieve lies in its restored 18th- to 19th-century remnants, including a brick belle of a **Southern Hotel** ($80 and up; 573/883-3493), at 146 S. 3rd Street, one of the oldest hotels west of the Mississippi River. **Sara's Ice Cream** (573/883-5890), down toward the water at 124 Merchant Street, provides yet more tasteful distractions, with great handmade ice cream cones, old-fashioned soda fountain drinks, and milk shakes.

Since US-61 doesn't enter town, follow the small blue Tourist Information signs down to the old waterfront to find the area's historic places, and visit the **Great River Road Interpretive Center** (daily; free; 573/883-7097 or 800/373-7007) at 66 S. Main Street to learn about the town's past and present.

To head south, go north: the **Mississippi River–Modoc Ferry** (daily; $8; 573/883-7382) to Modoc, Illinois, is almost three miles out of town. Follow Main Street north until it dead-ends at the ferry landing. On the Illinois side, 12 rural crop-lined miles from the Modoc Ferry we rejoin the GRR, heading south on Hwy-3 toward Chester.

Kaskaskia, Illinois

Fifteen miles south of Sainte Genevieve, signposted off US-61, is old **Kaskaskia,** the first Illinois state capital and the only Illinois town now *west* of the Mississippi, thanks to an 1881 flood. "Town" is a generous overstatement: Originally consisting of only a church and a handful of farmhouses, the community has been all but washed away numerous times in its 250-year history. Cut off from the Missouri shore by huge levees and a swampy river channel, Kaskaskia is now a ghost town with an illustrious past: It was here, during the American Revolution, that George Rogers Clark and his tiny force of Kentucky **"Long Knives"** launched their attack against British control of the huge, formerly French territory between the Mississippi and Ohio River Valleys, a campaign so stunningly successful that it effectively doubled the size of the United States. After capturing Fort Kaskaskia (now across the river), the victorious Americans rang the 600-pound bell that hung in the French Catholic church; this bell, now in its own spartan iron-barred chapel, is called the Liberty Bell of the West.

Chester: Home of Popeye

The GRR neatly skips around **Chester,** "Home of Popeye," via a pleasant riverbank detour, returning to Hwy-3 on the downstream side of town. **Popeye** first appeared in print in 1929, and a memorial to local boy Elzie Segar, creator of the spinach-guzzling scrapping Sailor Man, stands in a picnic area beside the bridge to Missouri; if you miss it, you'll have to turn around on the other side of the Mississippi. As the story goes, Chester locals Frank "Rocky" Fiegel and William "Windy Bill" Schuchert

were the inspiration for Popeye the Sailor and Wimpy the Hamburger Fiend. If you pass through on the second weekend of September, drop by Popeye's birthday party, with its big flea market of all the Popeye collectibles you never imagined existed.

Hwy-3: Shawnee National Forest

No town of any consequence impedes the GRR's 90-mile leg along the southern tip of Illinois. The roadside landscape continues to be fields of heat-loving corn and leafy soybean, while the bluffs of the Shawnee National Forest appear to the east. Much of the

Absentminded and lead-footed drivers beware: Some cash-strapped counties of southern Illinois are known to use speed traps to help make ends meet.

forested uplands are a botanical crossroads: glacier-borne northern species like the sumac and partridge berry; warmth-seeking southern species like the short-leaf pine; eastern species held back by the Mississippi, such as Virginia willow and silver bell; and western species with a toehold in the east, like Missouri primrose and Ozark coneflower. All count southern Illinois as the edge of their natural ranges. When John James Audubon passed through this region in the early 1800s, he recorded seeing thousands of bright green, red, and yellow-striped parakeets, but these birds are all long extinct.

Jonesboro

Just under 50 miles south of Chester, eight miles east of the GRR via Hwy-146, the small town of **Jonesboro** hosted the third of seven 1858 U.S. Senate campaign debates between challenger Abe Lincoln and incumbent Stephen Douglas, who tried to portray Lincoln as being out of touch with the people over the issue of slavery. Although Illinois was a designated free state, this area had strong sympathies with the South, something it maintains to this day. For proof, enjoy the down-home ambience and delicious smoked pork barbecue at **Dixie Barbecue,** 205 W. Broad Street (618/833-6437).

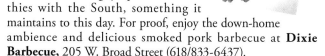

Broad Street, a.k.a. Hwy-146, roughly marks the route of the **Trail of Tears,** the 1838 winter death march of the Cherokee Nation. Six years after wiping out Indians of the upper Mississippi in the Black Hawk War, President Andrew Jackson ordered the "Five Civilized Tribes" of the Cherokee removed to the arid plains of Oklahoma from their fertile lands in north Georgia and eastern Tennessee, where gold had just been discovered. Some 5,000 Cherokee died along this 1,000-mile journey, which passed through the state near here. On the Missouri side of the river, 10 miles north of Cape Girardeau, the 3,400-acre **Trail of Tears State Park** (573/290-5268) preserves one scene along this marathon tragedy, with a two-mile section of the historic trail and interpretive plaques marking the wooded, riverside bluffs.

Cape Girardeau, on the Missouri side of the Mississippi River, was the boyhood hometown of radio talk-show host Rush Limbaugh, whose father and grandfather were local lawyers.

Back on Hwy-3, just north of I-57 and the town of Cairo, the GRR passes **Horseshoe Lake Conservation Area,** an example of what happens when the river shifts to a new channel and leaves an oxbow lake behind. Now prime winter habitat for over a million migrating geese and ducks, its tupelo gum trees, bald cypress, and swamp cottonwoods foreshadow the scenery found downstream among the bayous of the Mississippi Delta.

Cairo

"A grave uncheered by any gleam of promise" was but one of Charles Dickens's unsympathetic descriptions of **Cairo** (CARE-oh or "K"-ro, pop. 3,632), the town that presides over—and sometimes under—the meeting of the Mississippi and Ohio Rivers. Routinely submerged by floodwaters until the Corps of Engineers ringed the town with a massive stockade of levees and huge steel floodgates, Cairo's star shone briefly in the steamboat era and during the Civil War, when General Grant quartered his Army of the Tennessee here and Union ironclads were berthed along the waterfront. If you enjoy studying historic buildings (more often than not in Cairo, empty, decaying buildings), you can see many signs of the prosperity that helped Cairo reach a peak population of over 15,000 people: a number of Victorian-era mansions built by merchants and boat captains remain in varying stages of repair, there's a majestic public library, and volunteers have been slowly restoring the stately, circa-1872 **Customs House,** 1400 Washington Avenue (618/734-1019), into an intriguing (if incomplete) museum.

Along with the historic remnants, Cairo has something else worth seeing: the confluence of the two mighty rivers. Unless there's a flood in progress, do your watching from a small platform in **Fort Defiance State Park,** at the foot of the bridge that carries US-60 between Missouri and Kentucky, lasting but a quarter mile in Illinois.

Metropolis: Home of Superman

The town of Metropolis, Illinois (pop. 6,700), along the Ohio River 25 miles northeast of Cairo but most easily accessible via Paducah, Kentucky, takes pride in its adopted superhero son, Superman. An impressive and photogenic 15-foot-tall bronze statue of the Man of Steel stands downtown, on the north side of the Massac County Courthouse. Nearby are a quick-change telephone booth and the "offices" of the *Daily Planet* newspaper, and every June a festival celebrates his crime-fighting efforts. For more information, and a look at one of the most extensive collections of Superman artifacts and memorabilia anywhere, visit the

Metropolis, Illinois, the hometown of **Superman,** is also associated with another famous figure: Robert F. Stroud, the **"Birdman of Alcatraz,"** is buried in the Masonic Cemetery.

Super Museum (daily; $5; 618/524-5518) at 517 Market Street.

The other big attraction is the 40,000-square-foot **Harrah's Metropolis Casino,** down on the banks of the Ohio River at the base of the railroad bridge.

KENTUCKY
AND TENNESSEE

Most of the GRR's 60-odd miles across Kentucky are quite scenic, populated by only a handful of small towns, none of which has been overrun by tacky commercial strips. Continuing south across the Tennessee line, the route retains its rural, slow-road feel as it winds along the cultivated bottomlands around earthquake-created Reelfoot Lake. Midway to Memphis, the GRR comes back to the modern world, crossing the I-55 freeway then rejoining four-lane US-51 as it races to downtown Memphis, passing pine woods and cotton fields mixed with mobile homes, suburban ranch houses, and gas stations that double as the local video stores.

Wickliffe, Hickman, and the New Madrid Earthquake

Skipping from the banks of the Ohio River, the GRR stays with US-51 southbound through small, thoroughly industrial **Wickliffe** (pop. 794), then takes an attractive 40-mile meander away from the rivers through wooded hill country, returning to the edge of the Mississippi at **Hickman,** a dozen miles from the Tennessee line.

West from Hickman, there's a small ferry to Missouri, landing near the town of **New Madrid** (MAD-rid), where one of the strongest earthquakes ever to hit the United States struck on December 16,

In Search of Elvis

Scratch the surface of Memphis, and you'll always turn up a little Elvis, like pennies and pocket lint in an old sofa. That guy behind the counter? His mom used to give piano lessons to Elvis's stepbrothers. That woman at the next table? Her after-school job was in the Libertyland amusement park, which Elvis would rent out in its entirety just so he could ride the Zippin' Pippin' roller coaster for hours on end. A frequent Graceland visitor during the Elvis years collected fuzz from the shag carpet to give to friends; maybe the woman paying for her coffee still has her tuft. Even the owner of the greasiest old pizza joint will tell you how Elvis would come in with his band, "back when he was nothin.'" Get used to it: Elvis is everywhere.

The font of all this meta-Elvisness is, of course, **Graceland** (daily; 901/332-3322 or 800/238-2000), at 3734 Elvis Presley Boulevard (US-51) about a mile south of I-55 amid a clutter of burger joints and muffler shops. At age 21, flush with his early success, Elvis paid $100,000 for Graceland, which was one of the more fashionable houses in Memphis in 1957, and seeing what happens when Elvis's poor-white-boy taste and Hollywood budget run amok is well worth the price of admission. You can buy tickets to each part of the Graceland complex, or splurge on a $34 combination "Platinum Tour" ticket that gives admission to the mansion as well as the other "collections," such as the King's private jet or his car collection. (Many of his cars, including his famous pink 1955 Cadillac, are arrayed as if at a drive-in movie—with a big screen playing his race car scenes from *Viva Las Vegas* on a continuous loop—it's my favorite stop in the whole shebang.)

A visit to Graceland says very little about Elvis's music (though there is a room showing off an 80-foot wall full of gold and platinum records) but speaks volumes about his mystique. Elvis is buried on the property, alongside his father and mother, in the Meditation Garden.

Memphis

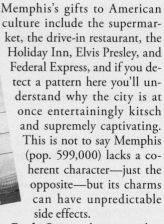

Memphis's gifts to American culture include the supermarket, the drive-in restaurant, the Holiday Inn, Elvis Presley, and Federal Express, and if you detect a pattern here you'll understand why the city is at once entertainingly kitsch and supremely captivating. This is not to say Memphis (pop. 599,000) lacks a coherent character—just the opposite—but its charms can have unpredictable side effects.

Beale Street, downtown between 2nd and 4th Streets, has been Memphis's honky-tonk central ever since native son W. C. Handy set up shop in the early 1900s with the blues he'd learned in Mississippi. Beale Street, and much of downtown Memphis, has been sanitized for your protection, turning it into a new! and improved! version of its old self, as a massive shopping mall and flashy new arena for the Grizzlies basketball team has transformed the entire south side of downtown Memphis. Slap an adhesive name tag on your lapel and you'll fit right in with the tour bus crowds strolling at night along Beale Street's block of clubs—including **B. B. King's** at 147 Beale Street (901/527-5464), marked by a giant neon guitar.

Fortunately, a number of other music-related museums and attractions capture a more authentic Memphis: The original **Sun Records** studio (daily; $9.50; 901/521-0664), where Elvis, Johnny Cash, Roy Orbison, and many others recorded their historic tracks in the 1950s, is a short walk northeast at 706 Union Avenue. Even more satisfying for most music obsessives: the site of **Stax Records** studio (daily; $12; 888/942-SOUL), at 926 E. McLemore Avenue, now an excellent museum documenting the soulful impact of Sam & Dave, Otis Redding, Al Green, and other greats during the 1960s.

If there's one place that shouldn't be missed, it's the eloquent **National Civil Rights Museum** (closed Tues.; $13; 901/521-9699), at 450 Mulberry Street, south of Beale Street behind the restored facade of the Lorraine Motel, where Dr. Martin Luther King Jr. was assassinated in 1968. Aided by extensive video newsreels and life-sized dioramas, museum exhibits let you step as far as you like into the powerful history of the Civil Rights Movement. Across the street, disturbing displays about Dr. King's assassination are housed in the old rooming house where James Earl Ray fired the fatal shots.

On the north side of downtown Memphis, **Mud Island** is a real island in the middle of the Mississippi River, connected to downtown by a pedestrian bridge and a monorail. This 50-acre island holds a five-block-long mock-up of the Mississippi River, with the Gulf of Mexico played by a huge, 1.3-million-gallon public swimming pool. Also here: the excellent **Mississippi River Museum.**

Right in downtown Memphis, but just a step away from the majors, the **Memphis Redbirds** ($5–15; 901/721-6050), Class AAA farm club for the St. Louis Cardinals, play at AutoZone Park at 200 Union Avenue.

Practicalities

As it is with live music, food is one area where Memphis can still surpass just about any other American city, and if your taste buds prefer improvisation and passion to over-refined "perfection," Memphis is sure to satisfy. Competition among the city's many rib shacks is fierce. Elvis Presley's favorite barbecue joint, **Charlie Vergo's Rendezvous** (901/523-2746), right downtown at 52 S. Second Street, with its main entrance through a downtown alley, is now something of a tourist trap. Main challengers to the title of "Best Barbecue in the Universe" include **Interstate BBQ** (901/775-2304), at 2265 S. 3rd Street, just north of where US-61 crosses I-55; and barebones drive-up BBQ stand **Cozy Corner** (901/527-9158), just east of US-51 at 745 North Parkway. For a change of pace

continued on next page

Memphis (continued)

from ribs, try the onion rings, burgers, beers, and live blues at another Memphis institution, **Huey's** (901/527-2700), right downtown at 77 S. 2nd Street.

Except during the city's many music and food festivals, Memphis accommodations are priced very reasonably. The whole alphabet of major chains—from Best Western to Super 8—is spread around the I-240 beltway, and again along I-55 in neighboring Arkansas. One landmark place to stay, the **Peabody Hotel,** 149 Union Avenue ($225 and up; 901/529-4000 or 800/732-2639) is Memphis's premiere downtown hotel, whose sparkling lobby is home to the Mississippi's most famous mallards: Twice daily, at 11 AM and 5 PM, the red carpet is rolled out for the Peabody Ducks to parade (waddle, really) to and from the lobby fountain. And if you're planning a vigil at Graceland, consider **Elvis Presley's Graceland Motel,** 3677 Elvis Presley Boulevard ($65–95; 901/332-1000 or 800/945-7667). Owned by his heirs and across from his former lair, it features a 24-hour in-room Elvis movie channel.

For tourist information contact the friendly and thorough **Memphis Convention and Visitors Bureau,** 47 Union Avenue (901/543-5300 or 800/873-6282), or drop by its information booth at 340 Beale Street.

1811. Seismographs and the Richter scale weren't around to measure it, but the quake was felt as far away as Boston.

Reelfoot Lake Area

Leaving Kentucky, the GRR follows Hwy-78 across a 40-mile stretch of low-lying bottomlands, passing the roadhouse bars and bait shops near **Reelfoot Lake,** a 25,000-acre recreation area and wildlife refuge created by the New Madrid earthquake. At **Dyersburg** (pop. 17,452), self-described as "friendly, God-fearing and patriotic citizens living and enjoying big city conveniences," the Great River Road jumps on to US-51, and from here south to Memphis the route does its level best to mimic an interstate, rendering the final 75 miles a forgettable blur.

Driving Across Memphis

Fans of pop-culture kitsch will love what the GRR offers in Memphis: The main road from the north (US-51) is Danny Thomas Boulevard; south of downtown, this turns into Elvis Presley Boulevard, and runs right past the gates of Graceland. (However, if you're continuing on to the Mississippi Delta, from Graceland you should switch onto US-61, which runs about two miles to the west.)

MISSISSIPPI

Ecologically speaking, the Mississippi Delta is the vast alluvial plain between Cairo and the Gulf of Mexico, but "The Delta" of popular myth is much more circumscribed, occupying the 250-mile-long realm of King Cotton, between Memphis and Vicksburg. As important as its proper boundaries is its legacy as the cradle of nearly every American musical style from gospel, blues, and jazz to country and rock 'n' roll. The backbone of our route, US-61, is also legendary as the path of the "Great Migration," the mass exodus to the industrialized northern United States of some five million black sharecroppers in the decades after World War I.

As the Great River Road cuts inland and drops like a plumb line across the cotton fields, we recommend a number of side trips to landmarks of this rich cultural heritage. Where the Delta ends at Vicksburg's bluffs, our route begins mingling with ghosts from the South's plantation and Civil War past, then finally rolls into Louisiana.

The word Mississippi comes from the Algonquin word *misezibi* meaning "water from land all over," or "great water."

Turn off the GRR toward Sam's Town and the Commerce Landing casinos to find the vestiges of **Robinsonville,** hometown of musician Robert Johnson, who according to blues legend traded his soul to Satan at "The Crossroads" of Highways 49 and 61 to become king of the blues guitar. In Johnson's day, of course, any guitar-pickin' "musicianer" was thought to be in cahoots with the Devil.

All across Mississippi, away from the main roads on the sleepier section of the GRR, the towns are filled with shotgun shacks, low-slung Creole-style bungalows, and old trailers that some people have nicknamed "doghouses" without any attempt at irony. What look like oil drums mounted on garden carts in the odd front yard are smokers, for doing barbecue just right; their presence sometimes implies the proximity of a social club or juke joint that may do only weekend business. Local stores, if they exist, are where men in overalls sit and stand in clusters, keeping an eye on the world. In autumn when the cotton is ready for harvest, huge truck-sized bales sit in the cleared muddy margins of the fields, and white fluff accumulates in drifts on the narrow loose shoulder, swirling in small eddies in your wake.

Meanwhile the Mississippi River does its snaky shuffle off to the Gulf of Mexico behind a continuous line of levees, a bayou here and cut-off lake there as proof of past indirections.

Northwest Mississippi: Casino Country

Leaving Memphis via US-61, the GRR enters De Soto and Tunica Counties; the place-names memorialize Hernando de Soto, the first European to see the Mississippi, and the combative Tunica tribe who forced the Spanish conquistador's mosquito- and snake-bitten expedition to flee across the river hereabouts in 1542. Outfitted with cannons, priests, slaves, pigs, war dogs, and 1,000 soldiers, de Soto spent years marching through southern swamps in quest of gold—but he was 450 years too early. Tunica County, long one of the most destitute places in America, only became a gold mine after the state legalized gambling in 1992. Several billion dollars of investment later, Tunica is the third-largest gambling center in the country, and every big name in the casino business lines the levee

Mississippi law doesn't require casinos to be riverboats, it merely requires them to float. All appearances to the contrary, the giant Las Vegas–style casinos in Tunica County are indeed floating, mostly in ponds dredged specifically to meet the letter of the law.

here. Bugsy Siegel would be proud, but as ever outsiders have benefited much more than the still-poor local residents.

To aid the influx of people anxious to part with their money, US-61 has been turned into a high-volume, four-lane highway. And motels, fast-food places, and gas stations have popped up like mushrooms after a spring rain.

One non-gaming benefit of all this investment has been the construction of the **RiverPark,** where a two-mile hiking trail winds through Mississippi wetlands, a real riverboat shuttles out onto the Mississippi for an hour-long cruise ($15), and a rooftop gallery gives grand views over the river.

South of the casino area along US-61, the GRR brings you to another traditional Mississippi experience: the classic grits-and-gravy, steak-and-potatoes **Blue & White Café,** at 1355 N. US-61 (662/363-1371). Offering a true taste of the Delta with its buffets and local specialties, including deep-fried pickles, the Blue and White has hardly changed since the day it opened in 1937. South from Tunica, US-61 makes a 35-mile beeline through the cotton fields to Clarksdale.

Moon Lake

Twenty miles south of Tunica's casinos, just west of US-61, **Moon Lake** was home to one of the South's most famous Prohibition landmarks, the Moon Lake Club. Unlike speakeasies associated with thugs and tarts, this club was a family destination where parents could dance and gamble while the kids played by the lake. In

a place and time when planes were still so rare the sound of their engines could interrupt work and empty classrooms, the club flew in fresh Maine lobster and Kansas City steak for its clientele of rich, white Memphians.

St. Louis likes to claim **Tennessee Williams** as a native son. While the family did indeed move there when Tom was in the fourth grade, the Mississippi-born playwright hated St. Louis "with a purple passion."

Moon Lake has a literary history, too, appearing in a number of Tennessee Williams's dramas. Williams knew it well: Not only was the club property owned by a cousin, but as a boy he had been a frequent guest, accompanying his grandfather, the Reverend Dakin, on parish calls throughout the county.

Now known as **Uncle Henry's Place** (662/337-2757), the restaurant is still popular, and cottages are sometimes available.

Helena, Arkansas

About a dozen miles west of the GRR and Moon Lake via US-49 is **Helena, Arkansas,** the most deadly place on the river to Union regiments in the Civil War, stopped in their tracks by the festering malarial swamps that once surrounded the town. It began building a different reputation back in the 1940s when local radio station KFFA 1360 AM began broadcasting the *King Biscuit Flour Hour,* a live blues show, originally hosted by harmonica legend Sonny Boy Williamson; the show is still on the air every weeday at 12:15 PM. In early October, the **Arkansas Blues and Heritage Festival** attracts fans by the tens of thousands to hear one of the best lineups of live gospel and blues in the nation. The **Delta Cultural Center** (daily; free; 870/338-4350), at 141 Cherry Street in the renovated train depot downtown, with its fine historical displays on the lives of Delta inhabitants, is an equally compelling reason to visit this small river town.

Clarksdale

The blues were born in the Delta, but they grew up in **Clarksdale.** The census rolls for this small town read like a musical hall of fame: Ma Rainey, W. C. Handy, Bessie Smith, Sam Cooke, Ike Turner, Muddy Waters, Wade Walton, John Lee Hooker, Big Jack Johnson, and many others whose achievements are described—and may be heard—in the **Delta Blues Museum** (closed Sun.; $7; 662/627-6820) in the circa-1918 railroad depot at the heart of Clarksdale's "Blues Alley" district downtown. The museum offers maps of blues landmarks around town and around the state, a calendar of blues events, and all sorts of helpful information. In short, this is the best place to start your journey through the Delta blues world.

Thomas Harris, author of *The Silence of the Lambs,* hails from the tiny hamlet of **Rich,** just east of the junction of US-61 and US-49.

Unlike the spreading deltas of the Orinoco or Nile, the Mississippi cuts a deeper channel as it rolls south, the deceptively smooth surface hiding a flow four times greater than it was at the St. Louis Arch.

Ever since W. C. Handy traded his steady gigs in Clarksdale for a career on Beale Street in Memphis, the Mississippi Delta has exported its blues musicians to places where they receive wider recognition and a living wage, but come on a Friday or Saturday

Getting the Blues

If serious blues hounds sniff around enough, they can still find the kind of swaggering, sweaty, Saturday-night juke joint that will always be synonymous with real Delta blues. You know the place: bottles of Budweiser on ice in a plastic cooler, clouds of cigarette smoke, some rough customers, hot dancing, and honest gut-wrenching blues played with an intensity that rattles your fillings. Yes, such places exist, but they don't run display ads in the local paper, or make the list of area attractions given out by local chambers of commerce.

The really homegrown variety announces itself with hand-lettered signs on telephone poles and launderette bulletin boards, if at all. They have no phone numbers and no advance tickets (usually); you have to show up to find out who, if anyone, is playing. Ask around—the convenience store clerk or the person next to you at the barbecue counter. Keep in mind that the blues are rooted in a condition of the Delta's black community that is no

About 30 miles south of Clarksdale on US-49 is **Parchman,** infamous home to the state prison farm memorialized in songs like bluesman Bukka White's "Parchman Farm." The "Midnight Special," another oft-heard allusion in Delta blues lyrics, was the weekend train from New Orleans that brought visitors to the prison.

night and you'll see Clarksdale still cooks up some good hot blues. Many of the most "authentic" juke joints are in dilapidated parts of town. For a first stop try the **Ground Zero Blues Club** (662/621-9009), a block from the Delta Blues Museum. If you're in town during August, it would be a shame to miss the **Sunflower River Blues and Gospel Festival,** organized by the Delta Blues Museum and staged at venues around town.

The rest of downtown Clarksdale is well worth exploring for its lazy ambience and wealth of history. The old **Delta Cinema,** downtown at 11 3rd Street, still shows current releases in a 1920s theater; there's a steamboat-

bed of roses; voyeurs slumming as tourists-to-hardship will be politely stonewalled at best. Rest assured, though: with perseverance and the proper attitude (and especially for women, a companion), you'll find what you're looking for. Once you get there, out-of-towners needn't worry about the reception: Blues musicians welcome an appreciative audience, period.

Weekends, again mostly Saturday nights, are also about the only time you'll catch blues in the more commercial juke joints and clubs, simply because so many musicians have other jobs during the week. If you really want to be sure of hearing some blues, time your travels to coincide with one of the big annual blues festivals, like these:

Sunflower River Blues and Gospel Festival
mid-August; Clarksdale, MS

Memphis Music and Heritage Festival
Labor Day weekend; Memphis, TN

Mississippi Delta Blues Festival
mid-September; Greenville, MS

Arkansas Blues and Heritage Festival
early October; Helena, AR

shaped store around the corner, across the street from the Sunflower River; and funky art galleries like **Cat Head Blues and Folk Art** (662/624-5992), at 252 Delta Avenue, showcase local culture and events.

Clarksdale has plenty of fast food, but the barbecue is better: Try the **Ranchero** (662/624-9768), on US-49 at 1907 N. State Street, or **Abe's Bar-B-Q** (662/624-9947), at 616 State Street in the center of town, cooking up tangy 'cue and pork-filled hot tamales since 1924. For a surprising (and comparatively healthy) dose of Lebanese-Italian food (and fantastic chocolate cream pies!) amid the pork palaces, check out **Chamoun's Rest Haven** (closed Sun.; 662/624-8601) at 419 N. State Street, on US-49 just south of the Big Sunflower River.

US-61, a.k.a. State Street, is also where you'll find

Clarksdale's motels, including **Comfort Inn** ($65; 662/627-5122) at the southern end of town. More adventurous visitors might want to consider Clarksdale's old Afro-American Hospital, where blues vocalist Bessie Smith died in 1937 after a car wreck out on US-61. Now called the **Riverside Hotel,** it rents a few minimally updated rooms at 615 Sunflower Avenue ($40; 662/624-9163). For a more comfortable but still definitely down-to-earth Delta experience, spend the night in a renovated sharecropper shack at the one-of-a-kind **Shack Up Inn** ($75 and up; 662/624-8329), on the grounds of the historic Hopson Plantation 10 miles south of Clarksdale. The half dozen wooden shacks have plumbing and power but still feel authentic, and you get your own front porch to practice your blues harp or simply take in the Delta dawn.

Oxford

Do you need a break from the Delta yet? Has counting pick-up trucks, propane tanks, and barbecued ribs induced a bad imitation drawl? How far would you detour for a well-stocked bookstore, or a restaurant that doesn't immerse everything in boiling oil? Sixty-two miles east of Clarksdale on Hwy-6 is the college town of **Oxford,** whose cultural amenities, though common to college towns from Amherst to Berkeley, set it in a world apart from most of Mississippi. The college in question is "Ole Miss," otherwise known as the **University of Mississippi,** whose pleasant campus holds such treasures as B. B. King's entire personal collection of records, posters, photos, and more in the **Ole Miss Blues Archive** (Mon.–Fri. only), in Farley Hall across from Barnard Observatory. The renovated antebellum observatory houses the **Center for the Study of Southern Culture** (Mon.–Fri. only; 662/232-5993), which sponsors exhibits, lectures, and screenings.

Elsewhere under the leafy old oaks you'll find a large collection of Southern folk art in the University Museums (closed Mon.), and a collection of William Faulkner first editions in the J. D. Williams Library. Faulkner was a resident of Oxford for most of his life; readers of his novels will recognize in surrounding Lafayette County (luh-FAY-it) elements of Faulkner's fictional Yoknapatawpha. A statue of him was recently placed in the square at the center of Oxford, and **Rowan Oak** (Tues.–Sat. 10 AM–4 PM, Sun. 1–4 PM; free; 662/234-3284), his house on Old Taylor Road off S. Lamar

Avenue, remains as he left it when he died in 1962, with the bottle of whiskey next to the old typewriter in his study almost, but not quite, empty.

Visit Faulkner's gravesite by following the signs from the north side of the courthouse square. Near the cemetery entrance lie other family members who didn't affect adding the "u" to their surname, including the brother whose untimely death Faulkner mourned in his first novel, *Soldier's Pay.*

Oxford Practicalities

When respects have been paid to Southern culture and it's time to eat, there's a lot to choose from. The central Courthouse Square is surrounded by good restaurants, ranging from the homespun **Ajax Diner,** at 118 Courthouse Square (662/232-8880; great pies & cobblers!), to the eclectic "New Southern" cuisine of the plush **City Grocery** (662/232-8080), at 152 Courthouse Square, where traditional dishes like bread pudding and shrimp and grits are complemented by fine wines and a full bar. And thanks to all the Ole Miss students, you can enjoy a range of fast food, pizza places, and live music along Lamar Street, south of the square.

Accommodations in Oxford include the **Downtown Oxford Inn and Suites** ($99 and up; 662/234-3031), a former Holiday Inn north of the courthouse at 400 N. Lamar, and the comfortably worn **Oliver-Britt House** ($80 and up; 662/234-8043), a redbrick, circa-1905 B&B at 512 Van Buren Avenue.

The **Oxford Tourism Council** (662/234-4680) will happily provide more information and a calendar of cultural events; it also operates a visitors center in a tiny cottage next to City Hall on the central square. Another good source of information is **Square Books,** on the south side of the same square. This is one of the country's great independent bookstores, with a full range of local and international authors, plus a nice café.

Hwy-1: Great River Road State Park

Between Clarksdale and Greenville, the Great River Road winds west of the much-busier US-61, looping next to the Mississippi River along Hwy-1. It's a

East of the GRR on Hwy-61 is small **Mound Bayou,** the oldest black town in the state. A man named Isaiah Montgomery, inspired by Booker T. Washington's prescriptions for black self-improvement, founded the all-black community in 1888 with support from his former employer, Jefferson Davis.

Across the Mississippi from Rosedale in a cotton field off Hwy-1 is **Rohwer, Arkansas,** where 8,500 Japanese Americans were forced from their California homes and imprisoned for the duration of World War II.

rural road, running past soybean, cotton, and "pond cat" farms—catfish farming is big business hereabouts. Midway along, the GRR runs past **Great River Road State Park,** near the town of Rosedale. Located inside the Mississippi River levee, the park offers unique views of the "Father of Waters" from a 75-foot-high overlook tower.

Farther south, at the north edge of Greenville, the 1,000-year-old, 55-foot-high earthen cones next to the highway are the remnants of the prehistoric "Moundbuilder" people who lived here a millennium ago. Now preserved as the **Winterville Mounds,** the two dozen ancient mounds here are thought to have been sacred ceremonial sites, but little is known about the enigmatic people who built them (and hundreds of others) along the banks of the Mississippi and Ohio rivers.

Greenville

The Delta's largest city, **Greenville** (pop. 41,633) is one of the largest river ports in the state, but instead of cotton-shipping wharves, its levees are now lined by floating casinos. Hwy-1 through Greenville takes top honors for the least attractive strip of gas stations and mini marts along the GRR, but appearances can be deceiving, as the city has some fine cultural traditions,

About 30 miles east of Greenville, **Moorhead** is known in blues geography as the place "where the Southern crosses the Dog," an allusion to the Southern and Yazoo-Delta (a.k.a. Yellow Dog) Railroads. Nearby **Money,** Mississippi, was the location of the notorious 1955 murder of 15-year-old Emmett Till, a key moment in the burgeoning Civil Rights Movement.

from the anti–Ku Klux Klan editorializing of Hodding Carter's *Delta-Democrat Times* during the 1950s and 1960s to the great steaks and hot tamales at **Doe's Eat Place** (662/334-3315). In the big white building at 502 Nelson Street (follow N. Broadway to the brick churches, then turn toward the river), Doe's is known throughout the state for its good food and honest prices, and for the fact that you have to enter through the kitchen. (Other Doe's Eat Place restaurants have opened around the South; the one in Little Rock, Arkansas, is a favorite of former president Bill Clinton.)

Second to Clarksdale in the Delta blues galaxy, Greenville comes alive in mid-September during the annual **Mississippi Delta Blues Festival** (662/335-3523 or 800/467-3582). For

Birth of the Teddy Bear

About 30 miles north of Vicksburg along US-61, the hamlet of **Onward** has a historical plaque marking the "birthplace of the Teddy Bear." The original Teddy Bear was inspired by a cub from the woods near Onward: Tied by a noose to a tree in the canebrakes, the cute fellow was found by President Teddy Roosevelt while hunting here in 1903. His refusal to shoot the defenseless animal, publicized in an editorial cartoon, garnered such popular approval that a New York firm requested the president's permission to name a stuffed toy after him. The only rub is, T. R. didn't actually refuse to shoot—because, in fact, he wasn't there. But neither was the cub! According to members of the hunting party, the president's guide, Holt Collier, an African American veteran of the Confederate cavalry, was challenged to prove he could lasso a bear. So he did, when one came along through the swamp—an old and rather weak one, as it turned out, that splashed around in a slough before they cut him loose. T. R., however, having tired of waiting for game, had returned to camp and missed the whole episode.

accommodations, look along US-82 near the junction with US-61, east of town.

Highway 61 Revisited

Between Greenville and Vicksburg, the GRR continues along Hwy-1 through the cotton-rich bottomlands, the landscape as unvarying as the country music that dominates the radio dial. Before the Civil War, this land was nearly unin-habitable hardwood forests and fever-riddled swamps, home to snakes, panthers, and mosquitoes. After Reconstruction, the valuable oaks, sweetgum, and hickory were logged off, the swamps drained, and levees built. Now just the snakes and

Hearing Delta blues live can be as big a challenge as finding it on the radio. Helena, Arkansas's historic **KFFA 1360 AM** plays at least an hour at lunchtime, and you can catch more contemporary music on Greenville's **WBAD 94.3 FM.**

mosquitoes remain. It's a long, slow ride, while US-61 races along to the east.

East of Greenville, just west of US-61, the town of Leland was the boyhood home of Muppet-master Jim Henson. There's now a small and suitably warm-spirited museum, on the north side of US-82 at Deer Creek, honoring him, Kermit the Frog, and his other creations.

The 50 miles of US-82 between Greenville and Greenwood pass through the heart of Delta blues country, and a number of nearby towns feature high on any "blues pilgrimage" itinerary: Holly Ridge holds the grave of **Charley Patton** ("Voice of the Delta," 1891–1934); Robert Johnson (1911–1938) is remembered by a burial marker in Itta Bena; B. B. King was born in Indianola and is honored in an annual festival the first weekend in June. Farther south on US-61, Rolling Fork was the birthplace of **Muddy Waters** (1915–1983), while the great bass player and songwriter Willie Dixon (1915–1992) was born in Vicksburg.

Vicksburg

The "Red Carpet City of the South," **Vicksburg** (pop. 26,407) didn't roll one out for the Union army during the Civil War. Instead, the city so stubbornly opposed Union efforts to win control of the Mississippi River that it became the target of one of the longest sieges in U.S. military history. After the war ended, Vicksburg suffered once again in 1876, when the city woke up to face a mud flat of flopping fish after the Mississippi River found itself a new streambed—overnight. Thanks to the diligence of engineers who redirected the Yazoo River in 1903, Vicksburg has its waterfront back, now complete with several modern-day sharks, whose slot machines and roulette wheels spin 24 hours a day for your entertainment.

To escape from Vicksburg's indoor onslaught of Chippendale claw feet, stop by **Margaret's Grocery** (601/638-1163), right on the GRR (old US-61) on the north side of town at 4535 N. Washington Street, where an assemblage of huge hand-lettered signs preach biblically inspired words of wisdom at passersby.

Many of the city's posh antebellum houses survived the Civil War with varying degrees of damage, and during the post-war Reconstruction several additional mansions were added to the bluffs overlooking the river. Most of these homes are open to the public (for

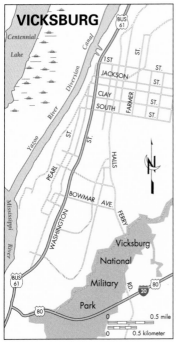

around $6 each), and during the fortnight-long "Pilgrimages" in late March and mid-October, slightly discounted multiple-house tours are available. The architecturally varied mansions, many of which double as B&Bs, and their copious inventories of fine antiques are more fascinating to decorative arts aficionados than to history buffs, who may find tours illuminating more for what is omitted than included. Stories of deprivation and Union plundering, cannonballs in parlor walls, and other wartime relics are religiously enshrined, yet only rarely is a word spoken about slavery.

The most famous of Vicksburg's antebellum homes is **Cedar Grove** (daily; 601/636-1000), south of downtown at 2200 Oak Street, which has a spectacular panorama over lush gardens and railroad yards down the bluffs to the broad Mississippi River. Ironically, Cedar Grove was built for a cousin of General Sherman, who used it as a military hospital. Another grand old mansion, **Anchuca** (601/661-0111), at 1010 E. 1st Street, preserves a more complete picture of antebellum life, with well-preserved gardens and slave quarters (plus a very fine café). Dozens more, dating from the 1870s up through the early 1900s, are found throughout Vicksburg's pleasant cobblestone residential areas.

The downtown commercial district, on the bluffs above the river, offers another, more contemporary glimpse into Southern culture. If you've ever tried to imagine a world without Coke, step into the **Biedenharn Coca-Cola Museum,** smack downtown at 1107 Washington Street, and see where one man's ingenuity slew all hopes for such a world. Here, in 1894, Joseph Biedenharn conceived of putting the strictly regional soda-fountain drink into bottles, the better to reach new markets.

The rest, as they say, is history. Toast worldwide domination with some of the classic stuff, straight up or over ice cream, or pay $3 to view galleries full of old promotional serving trays and the like.

Vicksburg National Military Park

Though the engineering feat that redirected the Yazoo and Mississippi Rivers, and brought Vicksburg more civil engineers per capital than any other U.S. city, is impressive, it's the story of the Civil War campaign to split the Confederacy in half that dominates history here. The battle for Vicksburg, which was known as the "Gibraltar of the Confederacy," reached its dramatic conclusion on July 4, 1863, amid the strategic heights and ravines of the 1,800-acre **Vicksburg National Military Park.** The ins and outs and strategizing behind the 47-day Siege of Vicksburg, and the story behind the 1,300-odd markers and monuments, becomes emotionally compelling after some accounting of the anecdotes of individual valor, of odd courtesies amid the bloodshed, and of the tragedy and humanity that lie behind the 16 winding miles of stone. The **visitors center** (daily; $8 per car; 601/636-0583), on the east side of Vicksburg via Clay Street or off I-20 exit 4, has exhibits, maps, brochures, and audio tours with narration and sound effects. Or, you can hire a guide to accompany you in your car and explain everything from battle tactics to the symbolism of the monuments. The advantage to a live guide is the opportunity to ask questions and to delve into whatever suits your curiosity, be it stories of the many women who fought incognito, or of the immigrants who enlisted to win citizenship.

While Vicksburg's surrender allowed President Lincoln to declare that "the Father of Waters now flows unvexed to the sea," local whites stayed vexed for over 80 years: Because the surrender occurred on July 4, until the end of World War II Independence Day in Vicksburg was celebrated only by African Americans.

One of the most unusual sights in the Vicksburg Military Park is the USS *Cairo,* an ironclad paddlewheel battleship that was sunk by a torpedo during the Civil War. Preserved for a century by the Mississippi mud, it was recovered and restored and is now on display in its own museum, above the river at the west end of the park.

Late in the year when the pecan crop is in, you can buy **pecans** from vans or shacks beside the highway. Buy pre-shelled ones, or spend hours struggling with a nutcracker.

Vicksburg also has two military cemeteries, one for each side. The Union cemetery is the largest Civil War burial ground in the country, holding the remains of more than 17,000 soldiers who died here and all over the south; more than 12,000 of the dead are simply marked "unknown." Another 5,000 Confederate dead are buried in the Vicksburg City Cemetery.

Vicksburg Practicalities

Vicksburg has an enormously compelling history, but it's also a very pleasant place to spend some time. For a traditional home-style feast, sit down to the communal round table at **Walnut Hills** (601/638-4910) at 1214 Adams Street and dig into the endless supply of classic regional dishes, from fried pork tenderloin to okra. Given the fresh ingredients (and depending on how much of a pig you can be), the moderate prices are a great value, and the overall ambience embodies the essence of Southern Hospitality. Deep-fried tamale addicts should seek out **Solly's Hot Tamales,** near the Cedar Grove mansion on US-61 Business at 1921 Washington Street (601/636-2020). Barbecue lovers will want to sample the offerings at **Goldie's Trail,** 4127 S. Washington Street (601/636-9839).

The icon of Southern gentility and refreshment, the mint julep, was allegedly born in Vicksburg: Water from fragrant **Mint Springs** in what is now the National Military Park was mixed with good Kentucky bourbon brought to town by riverboat captains. It goes without saying that Kentuckians and Tennesseeans consider this pure fiction.

You won't notice many people lolling about on grassy lawns or parks in the southern Delta, for the simple reason that this has become the realm of the **fire ant,** whose stinging bite would shame a wasp into adopting some other line of work.

Vicksburg motels, found at the south edge of town along I-20 between the Mississippi River and the Military Park, include a wide selection of the national chains and their local imitators; one of the nicest is the **Battlefield Inn** ($50–75; 601/638-5811), at the I-20/US-61 junction.

If you're in the mood, you can play Rhett and Scarlett for a night, pampering yourself with canopied beds in one of the dozen camellia-draped antebellum mansions (including Cedar Grove and Anchuca) that double as plush $150-a-night B&Bs. Any will have you whistling "Dixie," but true history buffs will want to request the Grant Room at Cedar Grove, which is still furnished with the very bed the general used after Union forces occupied Vicksburg. The staff claims Grant was a bedridden drunk for his entire stay, but pay no attention—he was probably a poor tipper at the bar, and folks around here bear grudges for generations over things like that.

For thorough information on lodging and attractions, contact the friendly **Vicksburg Convention and Visitors Bureau** (601/636-9421 or 800/221-3536) at 3300 Clay Street opposite the entrance to the National Military Park. If your visit falls during Pilgrimage, don't expect easy pickings on rooms: Most B&Bs are booked up to *two years* in advance for those weeks.

Port Gibson

For an overview of a nearly vanished Southern culture, spend some time at the **Museum of the Southern Jewish Experience** (601/362-6357). Based at a former Jewish summer camp in **Utica,** a half hour to the northeast of Port Gibson, the museum also has a branch exhibit in the basement of **Temple B'nai Israel** in Natchez, 213 S. Commerce Street (by appointment only; 601/362-6357).

One of the many little gems of the GRR is 30 miles south of Vicksburg: **Port Gibson,** the town General Grant found "too beautiful to burn." As they did with Savannah, Georgia, the Union Army spared Port Gibson during the Civil War, and decades of economic doldrums have spared the town from the Wal-Mart sprawl that at times seems to have enveloped the rest of the South. Fine homes still grace the pleasantly shaded main drag, but most eye-catching is the giant Monty Python prop known as the **Church of the Golden Hand** because its steeple is topped by a gold-leafed hand, its index finger pointing the way to Heaven. Actually, this is the circa-1859

"Church of the Golden Hand"

First Presbyterian Church, whose interior is lit by the gasoliers of the famous steamboat *Robert E. Lee,* the record-setting winner of the Great Steamboat Race of 1870. Newspapers of the day reckoned that millions of dollars were wagered on the outcome of the New Orleans-to-St. Louis race, which attracted international attention. The *Lee*'s three-day, 18-hour, and 14-minute victory was an upset for the favored title holder, the *Natchez.*

Across the street from the Golden Hand, next to an Exxon station, stands another unusual building, **Temple Gemiluth Chassed,** an elaborate Moorish-arched temple built in 1891 by Port Gibson's then large and prosperous Jewish community.

Ruins of Windsor and Emerald Mound

From Port Gibson, you can race along the 70-mph US-61 to Natchez, or follow a quietly scenic 50-mile detour along kudzu-lined country back roads and the serene Natchez Trace Parkway. The great Mississippi writer Willie Morris said "there is no more haunt-

Ruins of Windsor

ed, complex terrain in America" than this, and traveling through here you can't help but be aware of the region's many ghostly remnants. The looping first part of this route leaves Port Gibson next to the Exxon station, heading west on Rodney Road (Hwy-552) toward the Mississippi River past abandoned homesteads and picturesque old cemeteries rotting in the woods. After about 13 miles, look for a small sign and follow a short gravel road until you spot giant stone columns poking through the treetops. This is the **Ruins of Windsor.** Once the state's most lavish Greek Revival mansion and landmark to river pilots, it was reduced by an 1890 fire to its bare Corinthian ribs.

Another enigmatic remain is farther south, nearly invisible in the lush growth: **Emerald Mound,** a prehistoric platform over 400 feet wide and 35 feet tall. The second-largest mound in North America, it was built around 1250 AD and was still in use as a ceremonial center when the first Europeans arrived;

Emerald Mound is open daily, located on Hwy-553 just west of Natchez Trace Parkway milepost 10.3.

Natchez

Before the Civil War, **Natchez** (NATCH-iss, rhymes with "matches") had the most millionaires per capita in the United States, and it shows. If luxurious antebellum houses make your heart beat faster, Natchez (which has more than 500 antebellum structures inside the city limits), with its innumerable white columns and rich smorgasbord of Italian marble, imported crystal, and sterling silver, might just put you in the local ICU. That so much antebellum finery still exists is because Natchez, unlike Vicksburg, surrendered to Grant's army almost without a fight. Anti-Yankee sentiment may in fact run higher now than during the war, for Natchez was vehemently opposed to the Confederacy and outspokenly against Mississippi's secession from the Union. Since Natchez was second only to New Orleans as social and cultural capital of a region with two-thirds of the richest people in America, most of whom owed their wealth to slave-picked cotton, its support of the Union might seem a little incongruous.

Of course, such apparent contradictions should come as no surprise from a community raised with genteel cotillions and the Mississippi's busiest red-light district side by side. (Once-disreputable Natchez Under-the-Hill, where the most famous brothel in the South was destroyed by a fire in 1992, is today but a single gentrified block of riverfront bars and restaurants lined up alongside a permanently moored riverboat casino.

As befits the place that originated the concept, the annual Natchez Pilgrimages (held in late Spring, October, and at Christmas) are twice as long as the typical 10–15 days done elsewhere. The number of **antebellum mansions** open to the public more than doubles, hoop skirts and brass-buttoned waistcoats abound, and musical diversions like the Confederate Pageant are held nightly. Among the most fascinating homes open year-round is the one that didn't get finished: **Longwood,** on Lower Woodville Road, is the nation's largest octagonal house, capped by a red onion dome. Its grounds are fittingly gothic, too, with moss-dripping tree

Across the Mississippi from Natchez, the town of **Ferriday, Louisiana,** was where rocker **Jerry Lee "Great Balls of Fire" Lewis** and his cousins, country star Mickey Gilley and evangelist **Jimmy Swaggart,** grew up. Many items from the old Lewis home are on display at the **Delta Music Museum** at 218 Louisiana Avenue (daily; 318/757-9999).

Natchez Trace Parkway

A mile or so south of Port Gibson, US-61 and the GRR cross the much more relaxed Natchez Trace Parkway, which, like the Blue Ridge Parkway, is a scenic route managed by the National Park Service. The Parkway follows the route of the old Natchez Trace, a pre-Columbian Indian path that grew into the major overland route between the Gulf Coast and the upper Mississippi and Ohio River Valleys in the years before steamboats provided a faster alternative. The Natchez Trace appeared on maps as early as 1733, and from the 1780s to the 1820s, when steamboats made it obsolete, the Natchez Trace was one of the nation's most traveled routes. Farmers and craftspeople in the Ohio River Valley would transport their products by raft downstream to Natchez or New Orleans, then return on foot, staying at the dozens of inns along the route while doing battle with swamps, mosquitoes, and bands of thieves.

The entire 430-mile length of the Parkway, which runs from Nashville south to the edge of Natchez, with a short break around Jackson, is well paved and makes a delightful driving or riding route, with places of interest marked every few miles. Just north of Port Gibson at milemarker 41.5, the Sunken Trace preserves a deeply eroded, 200-yard-long section of the trail, the canopy of moss-laden cypress trees offering one of the most evocative five-minute walks you can imagine. Between Port Gibson and Natchez, sights along this short (and eminently bicycleable) stretch include the prehistoric **Emerald Mound,** the second-largest prehistoric structure in the United States, which dates from around 1400 AD and offers a commanding view of the woodlands. **Mount Locust** at milemarker 15.5 is a restored Trace roadhouse and the best place to pick up parkway information; if you're fortunate, you might get a tour guided by park ranger Eric Chamberlain, who was born in the house, and whose family lived there for five generations.

The National Park police keep the parkway under very thorough radar surveillance, by the way, so try to stay within the posted speed limit, often 35 mph with a maximum of 50 mph.

There are no cotton fields around Natchez, because all the cotton that paid for these mansions was grown across the river in the Louisiana bottomlands.

limbs, sunken driveway, and the family cemetery out in the woods. Information on the Pilgrimages, other house tours (about $8 per house), and the chance to stay in one of many historic B&Bs all comes from the same group, Natchez Pilgrimage Tours (601/446-6631 or 800/647-6742), which also runs horse-drawn carriage tours.

Southern history doesn't merely comprise those Greek Revival heaps and their *Gone With the Wind* stereotypes. Natchez, for example, had a large population of free blacks, whose story is told in downtown's **Museum of Afro-American History and Culture** (call for hours; 601/445-0728), in the old Post Office at 301 Main Street, where you'll also find interesting Black Heritage walking-tour brochures. Large Jewish sections in the **City Cemetery** (follow signs for the National Cemetery; City Cemetery is along the way) also furnish evidence of the South's tapestried past. The marble statuary and decorative wrought iron offer a pleasant outdoor respite for weary mansion-goers, too.

Natchez Practicalities

As befits a place with a strong tourism trade, Natchez has some great places to eat. Natchez is almost the southern extremity of the Tamale Belt, and you can sit down to a paperboard dish of them (a dozen for $6) at **Fat Mama's** (601/442-4548), 303 S. Canal Street. Fat Mama's also serves killer "Knock You Naked" margaritas, a combination which draws large crowds on summer nights (and earned the place a role in Jill Conner Browne's novel *Sweet Potato Queens' Book of Love*).

If you prefer fried catfish, po' boys, and chocolate shakes, head down to the **Malt Shop** (601/445-4843), where Martin Luther King Street (US-61 Business) dead-ends into Homochitto Street. For a change of pace, try **Pearl Street Pasta** (601/442-9284), just off Main Street at 105 S. Pearl Street, whose short, dinner-only menu is eclectic, reasonably priced, and laced with vegetables that haven't been boiled to oblivion.

One last Natchez landmark deserves special mention: **Mammy's Cupboard** (601/445-8957), a roadside restaurant in the shape of a five-times-larger-than-life Southern woman, whose red skirts house the small dining room and gift shop. Having survived many incarnations, Mammy's is once again open for business, offering home-made lunches (red beans and rice, sandwiches, iced tea served up in Mason Jars, and a huge range of scrumptious desserts) 11 AM–2 PM Monday–Saturday. Mammy's Cupboard can be found along the east side of four-lane US-61, roughly five miles south of down-town Natchez.

Mammy's Cupboard, Natchez

Accommodations in Natchez in-clude a half dozen familiar names scattered along US-61 and US-84 both north and south of down-town. For a more memorable expe-rience, consider staying the night in one of those historic mansions, many of which do double-duty as B&Bs. Top of the line is probably **Monmouth Plantation,** 36 Melrose Avenue ($175 and up; 601/442-5852), preserved as it was in its circa-1818 heyday and set amidst 25 acres of lush gardens. Keep in mind the enormous popularity of Pilgrimage requires seriously ad-vanced bookings during those times.

For an illustrated B&B guide and other useful information contact the **Natchez Convention and Visitors Bureau** (800/647-6724), which operates a large orientation center near the Mississippi River bridge (US-84) at 640 S. Canal Street.

Woodville: Rosemont Plantation

Rolling and curving past hay fields and woods, the distinc-tively red earth of southern Mississippi crowding the soft shoulders, the GRR passes quickly over the 45 miles between Natchez and the Louisiana state line. You won't see it from the highway, but just across the Mississippi is possibly the most significant piece of engineering anywhere along its length: the **Old River Project.** More than mere flood control, the project is designed to keep the Mississippi going down to Baton Rouge and New Orleans, rather than finding a new route to the Gulf via the Atchafalaya River. This actually happened during the 1948 flood, and there are hydrologists who predict it is only a matter of time before it will happen again—a po-tential economic catastrophe for downstream cities along both rivers. About 10 miles north of the border, an unprepossessing intersection of gas stations marks the turnoff west for **Woodville** (pop. 1,393), where a lovely old courthouse sits at the center of a green square full of stately old oak trees, and a trio of historic churches line the somnolent streets.

The biggest attraction of Woodville, however, is a mile east of the GRR on US-24, where a small sign along the highway marks the entrance to **Rosemont Plantation,** the boyhood home of Confederate President Jefferson Davis. Built in 1830 with wooden pegs holding together hand-hewn posts and beams, the house is surrounded by a grove of live oaks and a large rose garden, planted by Davis's mother, after which the plantation takes its name.

LOUISIANA

As the GRR approaches its southern end, land and river begin to merge. With giant levees on one side and standing water on the other, it's easy to imagine the land is sinking—and indeed, by the time you roll off elevated I-10 into New Orleans, you will be four to six feet *below* sea level.

From the St. Francisville ferry to the Interstate bridge just west of New Orleans, the GRR crosses the Mississippi four times, threading along rough back roads past a series of fine antebellum plantation homes along what's sometimes called **Plantation Alley.** The GRR also runs among a barrage of industrial giants whose toxic discharges have earned the region another sobriquet: Chemical Corridor. The Great River Road across Louisiana is not without its charms—a vividly painted church out in a field, or wrought iron gates framing exquisitely gnarled live oaks festooned with Spanish moss—but these are all too often overshadowed by the specter of a land being poisoned for profit. End of sermon.

St. Francisville

Louisiana is divided into parishes rather than counties, one of many subtle reminders of the original French Catholic settlement of the state. The past is ever-present in this part of the country, so turn west off US-61 at **St. Francisville,** and ex-

plore the myriad tales of this fascinating community, which grew up around the graveyard of a frontier-era monastery. Pick up an anecdotally rich walking-tour brochure at the **West Feliciana Historical Society Museum** (225/635-6330), at 11757 Ferdinand Street, for a sample of the architectural charms that draw visitors to this curious little town. All around St. Francisville, there are grand old manor homes, most notably at **Rosedown Plantation** (daily; $10; 225/635-3332), on Hwy-10 just east of US-61, where a 370-acre state-run historic site preserves an 1830s main house, a pair of slave cabins, and lush formal gardens. About five miles southeast of St. Francisville on Hwy-965, off US-61 at the Roadside BBQ stand, is the **Audubon State Historic Site** (daily; 225/635-3739) also known as the Oakley House, where in 1821 naturalist and illustrator John James Audubon came to work as a resident tutor while he compiled his comprehensive *Birds of America*.

Along with the rich history, St. Francisville also has one compelling, contemporary attraction: the **Magnolia Cafe** (225/635-6528), a wonderful little restaurant housed in the old 3V motor

A dozen miles west of St. Francisville and the Great River Road along Hwy-1, the small town of **Morganza, Louisiana,** was the place where the character played by Jack Nicholson was beaten to death in his sleeping bag in the classic 1960s road movie *Easy Rider.* North of St. Francisville via Hwy-66 is **Angola,** location of a state prison that holds a famous annual rodeo and Louisiana's Death Row, which was featured in the book and movie *Dead Man Walking.*

Greenwood Plantation, St. Francisville

court complex at the corner of Commerce and Ferdinand Streets. The café moved here when its original home (a gas station) burned down in 2003, but it's better than ever, still serving some of the best-tasting po' boys in the state that invented them. The Magnolia doubles as one of the coolest little nightclubs anywhere, drawing big-name alt-folk performers like Dave Alvin and the Bottle Rockets, who stop here in between big-city gigs. There's also a coffeehouse-cum-art gallery and occasional cabins for overnight guests; there's no better place to get a feel for this part of Louisiana.

Heading on from St. Francisville, race south down US-61 to Baton Rogue, or snake west along Ferdinand Street for about a mile until the road dead-ends at the large car ferry (on the hour and half hour; $1) that shuttles across the Mississippi toward Louisiana's legendary Cajun Country.

Baton Rouge

From the lofty vantage point of the I-10 bridge over the Mississippi River, **Baton Rouge** (pop. 227,818) appears to be a largely industrial city, its skyline dominated by smokestacks, a WW II destroyer, a mock–Mississippi Riverboat casino, and the nation's tallest state capitol—essentially a 34-story monument to the populist demagoguery of Huey "Kingfish" Long. Just south of the towering capitol, a life-sized animatronic figure of Long, the state's legendary Depression-era governor, dominates the **Old**

State Capitol (daily; $4), that clearly visible white Gothic-style castle—the only thing missing is a moat. Inside the restored 1847 edifice are engaging computer-aided history exhibits, including one about Huey Long's unresolved 1935

assassination: Was the patronage-dealing, road-building, vote-buying potentate the target of premeditated murder, or was then–U.S. Senator Long the victim of his five trigger-happy bodyguards' "friendly fire," aimed at a man who merely punched the boss? Review the evidence and draw your own conclusions.

Another lesson in Louisiana history can be yours at the wonderful **Rural Life Museum** (daily; $7; 225/765-2437), managed by Louisiana State University and located at 4600 Essen Lane, east of downtown off I-10 exit 160. This expansive collection of shotgun houses, barns, farming equipment, riverboats, donkey carts, hand tools, and appliances—basically, anything that might have been seen in the state 100 years ago—was assembled on a former plantation by artist Steele Burden. The rest of the plantation is now a picturesque garden that covers 25 acres.

Baton Rouge hosts the **Pennington Balloon Championship** early in August. Besides being a beautiful sight, the hundreds of colorful balloons take part in a target competition, trying to drop beanbags onto a bulls-eye from 1,000 feet in the air.

The popularity of college football shouldn't be underestimated in Baton Rouge: Motel No Vacancy signs light up all over town whenever the **LSU Tigers** play. Basketball, baseball, and other sports are big, too; for tickets, call LSU (800/960-8587).

Baton Rouge Practicalities

If you're looking for a place to eat and absorb a little Baton Rouge ambience, the **Pastime** (225/343-5490), a few blocks from the Old State Capitol at 252 South Boulevard, right under the I-10 interchange, is one of those windowless, smoky sports bars ideally suited for discussing political chicanery over po' boys, fried fish, and beer. Best pizzas in town, too—try the one topped with crawfish tails for some local flavor. Another excellent place to eat a fine meal and get filled in on local life ways is world-famous **Jay's Barbecue,**

Along with po' boys and boiled crawdads, Louisiana's roadsides offer another local specialty, the **daiquiri bar.** Like a high-octane version of a Dairy Queen slush, daiquiris come pre-mixed in a variety of sticky fruit flavors and sizes up to an eye-crossing 32-ouncer. Most of these bars have drive-up windows: In the eyes of the law, that piece of masking tape across the cup's lid makes it a "sealed container," so it's legal to drive with one in your cupholder, as long as you don't insert the straw.

Louisiana is divided into **parishes** rather than counties, one of many subtle reminders of the original French Catholic settlement of the state.

5734 S. Sherwood Forest Boulevard (225/293-1232), open every day but Sunday for real good ribs, pulled-pork sandwiches, hickory burgers, po' boys—and, if you're lucky and ask nicely, smoked alligator.

Another bunch of good eating and drinking prospects are clustered around the Highland Avenue entrance to Louisiana State University, a couple of miles south of I-10. **Louie's Cafe** (225/346-8221), at 209 W. State Street across from the Super Fresh shopping plaza, is open 24 hours, so there's no excuse to miss it. Facing the LSU gates at 3357 Highland is **The Chimes** (225/383-1754), a restaurant and oyster bar with 100 beers from 24 countries and frequent live music. Several other bars in the vicinity offer music with some regularity, but be warned that undergraduate projectile vomiting is a serious hazard.

While there are a number of hotels in downtown Baton Rouge, and along the highways south and east of town, most of the inexpensive accommodations cluster around exit 151 on I-10, two miles west of the Mississippi in Port Allen. For a memorably characterful overnight, try **The Stockade B&B**, 8860 Highland Road ($135 and up; 225/769-7358), a home-style inn on spacious grounds near LSU.

Cajun Country

West of New Orleans and Baton Rouge, a world away from the grand houses of lining the Mississippi River, the watery world known as Cajun Country spreads along the Gulf of Mexico. If you have the time to explore, the region offers an incredible range of delights for all the senses: antebellum plantation houses and moss-covered monuments set amidst groves of stately old oak trees, with all manner of wildlife (from birds to gators) chirping and squawking away in the oddly still bayous, and the sound of accordions and the aroma of boudin sausages and boiling crawfish emanating from what can seem like every other doorway. Cajun Country is also sugarcane country: Over half a million acres are cultivated each year, rising to 10 feet in height by the end of summer, when the cane is chopped down and made into molasses at the many aro-

The bridge that now carries US-190 over the Mississippi was built during the gubernatorial reign of the notorious **"Kingfish," Huey P. Long.** The structure was designed to be low enough to prevent oceangoing freighters from passing, thus snuffing out the chances of Vicksburg and other upstream cities to compete with the port of Baton Rouge—now the nation's fifth-busiest.

matic mills. The name "Cajun" comes from the French-speaking Catholic Acadians, 10,000 of whom were chucked out of Canada when the English took over in 1755. The Acadians were refused entry by the American colonies on the East Coast and had to make their way to this corner of still-French Louisiana, where they absorbed many other cultural influences while retaining their distinct identity.

US-90, the main route through Cajun Country, follows the route of the Old Spanish Trail, the historic cross-country highway that, in the early days of the automobile, linked San Diego and St. Augustine. Though the main route has been widened and "improved" countless times in the past century (it is often signed as Future I-49), many wonderful stretches of old country road still wind along shady bayous. Wandering aimlessly, getting lost amidst the many small backwater towns is half the fun of spending time here, but there are a number of places where the whole Cajun Country experience comes together in a concentrated dose. One of your main stops should be the historic town of **St. Martinville,** where the **Church of St. Martin de Tours,** 103 Main Street ($1; 337/394-7334), stands at the center of many blocks of ornate buildings and majestic oak trees, including the one featured in the Cajun-flavored Longfellow poem "Evangeline." St. Martinville is just north of **New Iberia,** the home of Tabasco sauce, perhaps Cajun Country's most identifiable product, and just south of another great stop in Cajun Country: **Breaux Bridge,** the "Crawfish Capital of the World," located just off the I-10 freeway, a quick half hour west of Baton Rouge. Next to the bridge in Breaux Bridge, look for **Café des Amis,** 140 E. Bridge Street (337/332-5273), renowned for its Saturday morning Zydeco Breakfast. The music, with a full band, starts bright and early (usually around 8:30 AM).

Plantation Alley

Between Baton Rouge and New Orleans, if you don't have a stomach strong enough to bear miles of industrial blight, hop onto the I-10 freeway, but if your senses can handle the constant juxtaposition of refined domestic design alongside unsightly industrial complexes, with a few trailer parks, upscale vacation homes, and photogenic above-ground cemeteries thrown in for good measure, the Great River Road is full of treats, and this 100-mile traverse of what is promoted as Plantation Alley may well be a highlight of your trip. To

New Orleans

Royal Street in the French Quarter

Long famous for its easygoing, live-and-let-live personality, and for placing a high value the good things in life—food, drink, and music, to name a few—New Orleans was shocked by the destruction that followed in the wake of Hurricane Katrina in 2005. Slowly but surely, the Big Easy continues to recover from the 2,000 deaths and over $100 billion worth of damage. No one who knows and loves New Orleans can have any doubt that the city will get its groove back before too long.

With deep roots going back to the earliest days of European settlement in North America, New Orleans is very proud of its multicultural heritage: Its people, its ornate buildings, and especially its food all reflect a uniquely diverse and resilient culture. The focus of New Orleans, for visitors and locals alike, is the **Vieux Carré,** in the French Quarter, which sits on the highest ground in the city and thus escaped the worst of Katrina's floods. Centering on Bourbon Street, lined with tacky souvenir stalls and strip clubs catering to conventioneers, this square mile is full of wrought-iron balconies on picturesque brick buildings. Yes, it's a huge tourist attraction, but it's also the heart of old New Orleans. At the center of the quarter is **Jackson Square,** where a statue of the victor of the Battle of New Orleans, Andrew Jackson, stands in front of St. Louis Cathedral, which was rebuilt in 1850 on top of an original foundation dating back to 1724. The nearby **Old U.S. Mint** (closed Mon.; $6; 504/568-3660), at 400 Esplanade, has the famous "Streetcar Named Desire" on display in the courtyard and holds excellent collections tracing the history of two New Orleans institutions: jazz and Mardi Gras.

After dark, there's live music aplenty in all styles and modes, but one stop you have to make is **Preservation Hall,** 726 St. Peter Street (nightly from 8 PM; $10; 504/522-2841), for the redolent ambience and the live traditional Dixieland jazz, still going strong after nearly 50 years.

Practicalities

New Orleans has some of the best and most enjoyable places to eat in the world, so plan to take the time to enjoy yourself here. In the French Quarter, the informal **Acme Oyster House** (504/522-5973), at 724 Iberville Street, is the place to go for the freshest bivalves, but it closes early by New Orleans standards—around 10 PM nightly. At the other end of the spectrum is expensive, formal **Antoine's** (504/581-4422), at 713 St. Louis Street, one of the oldest restaurants in the world, serves classic French-Creole cuisine to a who's who of New Orleans society. Another very popular spot is **K-Paul's Louisiana Kitchen** (504/596-2530) at 416 Chartres Street, where Chef Paul Prudhomme, who popularized Cajun-style "blackened" food all over the country, saves the very best examples for his own place. Another world-famous place that merits a meal or two: **NOLA** (504/522-6652), at 534 St. Louis Street, a comparatively casual setting for celebrated chef Emeril Lagasse's finely crafted Creole fare.

No visit to New Orleans is complete without a stop for coffee and beignets (and some serious people-watching) at busy **Cafe du Monde** (504/525-4544), open 24 hours a day on the river side of Jackson Square at 813 Decatur Street. A wider range of beverages, and even more immersive history, is on tap at the legendary **Napolean House** bar, 500 Chartres Street (504/524-9752).

Except during Mardi Gras, Jazzfest, or Superdome football games, places to stay in New Orleans aren't *all* that expensive. In the French Quarter at 828 Toulouse Street, the characterful **Olivier House** ($125 and up; 504/525-8456) is a quirky, family-run hotel filling a pair of French Quarter townhouses. Another good bet: **Place d'Armes Hotel** ($150 and up; 504/524-4531 or 800/366-2743) at 625 St. Ann Street, right off Jackson Square at the heart of the French Quarter, with rooms facing onto a quiet courtyard.

The best visitor information is provided by the **New Orleans Metropolitan Convention and Visitors Bureau** (504/566-5011).

For a dramatic perspective, cross the Mississippi on the Hwy-70 **Sunshine Bridge,** which runs between the GRR at Donaldson and I-10 exit 182. A quick link between Plantation Alley and New Orleans, the Sunshine Bridge was named in honor of "Singing Governor" Jimmy Davis's most famous song, "You Are My Sunshine," now the state's official song.

19th-century passengers aboard the packet steamboats traveling the lower Mississippi, the great mansions adorning the river bends between Baton Rouge and New Orleans must have made an impressive sight. The houses are no less grand today but, sadly, their surroundings have been degraded by the presence of enormous petrochemical refineries. These have, by and large, replaced the antebellum sugarcane fields as the region's economic engine, but in late summer when the cane is 10 feet tall and the smell of molasses fills the air, you can *almost* pretend nothing has changed.

Giving directions along Plantation Alley is complicated by the winding Mississippi, with its bridges and ferry boats, by the numerous roads and highways, and by the fact that the region is equally easy to explore from Baton Rouge or New Orleans, but it's as a good place as any to get lost and found again, so take your time and enjoy the ride. Below are four of the most popular and memorable plantation estates, but there are many along the way, in varying stages of restoration and decay.

Nottoway

Heading north to south, as the river flows, the first of these riverside manors is **Nottoway** (daily; $20; 225/545-2730), whose 64 rooms place it among the largest plantation homes in the South. Built in the 1850s, it was also one of the last "big houses" to be built. On the western shore of the Mississippi, along Hwy-1 about two miles north of the town of White Castle, Nottoway is a bright white Greek Revival structure enclosing over an acre of floor space, so you'll be glad you don't have to pay the air-conditioning bills or do the dusting. If you like the look of it all, you can stay for lunch in the grand dining room, or overnight in one of many lushly appointed rooms ($150–250).

Two miles south of White Castle, a state-run ferry jogs across the river (every 30 min., during commute hours only) to Carville on the other side.

Burnside: Houmas House

The most familiar (and easiest to reach) of Louisiana's plantation homes, **Houmas House** (daily; 225/473-9380), stands on the east bank of the Mississippi amid 12 acres of manicured grounds. Another of Louisiana's *grandes dames,* Houmas House is a dignified complex of buildings constructed over many generations, mainly between the 1780s and 1840s. The main is composed of white columns and rich red-ochre walls supporting a central belvedere (like a cupola) from which the antebellum owners could survey their domain. Today, the endless seas of sugarcane have been replaced in part by the monstrous sprawl of the neighboring DuPont plant. Once the seat of a massive, 20,000-acre sugarcane plantation, Houmas House may well look strangely familiar: The stately home was used as the setting for Robert Aldrich's 1965 gothic Southern horror film, *Hush, Hush, Sweet Charlotte,* starring Bette Davis, Olivia de Havilland, Joseph Cotten, and Bruce Dern. B&B rooms and a restaurant are also available.

Located at 40136 River Road (Hwy-942) near the hamlet of Darrow, Houmas House is just four miles west of the I-10 freeway via Hwy-22 or Hwy-44, and it is about a dozen miles north of the Sunshine Bridge (Hwy-70) over the Mississippi.

Driving along the river near Houmas House, you may pass the remains of another old plantation home, **Tezcuco,** which was built in 1855 and burned to the ground in 2002; all that remains are the chimneys and a number of outbuildings. Yet another local landmark, the 7,500-square-foot, 1820s-era **Bocage House,** was recently up for sale—for a cool $5.5 million.

Vacherie: Oak Alley and Laura

Traveling along the GRR, moldering concrete mausoleums, houses with loud colors and louvered French doors, insouciant pedestrians along the levee (not to mention the dangerously large potholes), all may arrest your attention briefly, but **Oak Alley** (daily; $20; 225/265-2151) will probably stop you in your tracks. This place is to antebellum plantations what Bora Bora is to islands, or the Golden Gate is to bridges: Even if you've managed to avoid seeing Oak Alley on tourist brochures, or in the movies *Interview with a Vampire* or *Primary Colors*, it will look familiar—or rather, it will look exactly like it ought to. Plus, no cooling tower or gas flare mars the immediate horizon. For the full effect of the grand quarter-mile-long allée of arching live oaks, which were planted in the 1700s, nearly a century before the current house was built in the late 1830s, drive past the entrance a short ways. Besides the obligatory tour, there's lodging and a restaurant in buildings on the grounds in back of the main house.

Oak Alley stands on the west bank of the river, three miles north of Vacherie at 3645 Hwy-18/Great River Road. The house is about 15 miles south of

Oak Alley

the Sunshine Bridge, and eight miles north of the Veteran's Memorial Bridge (Hwy-3213). There's a ferry nearby, too, between Edgard and Reserve, but this runs at very limited hours.

As a colorful antidote to the grand, whitewashed privilege on display at Oak Alley, set aside some time for a tour of nearby Laura plantation as well. Smaller, but seeming more in touch with the realities of sugarcane plantation life, **Laura** (daily; $18; 225/265-7690) presents itself as a Creole plantation and plays up the myriad of ethnicities and cultures that came together in Louisiana. Laura is nine miles downriver from Oak Alley, south of Vacherie at 2247 Hwy-18 (Great River Road).

Continuing south from Vacherie, scattered housing begins to invade the sugarcane, and traffic starts to pick up as the GRR (Hwy-18) works its serpentine way past a pair of ferry landings, a nuclear power plant, and a huge chemical plant with a photogenic cemetery felicitously occupying its front yard. By the time the GRR is within sight of the stylish, rusty-red I-310 bridge, the tentacles of New Orleans's bustle are definitely apparent. Hop on the Interstate eastbound, and inside of 25 miles you can be hunting for parking in New Orleans's Vieux Carré, or searching for a Sazerac to celebrate the journey.

Driving New Orleans

Assuming you resisted the industrial-strength charms of US-61 and opted to take the I-10 freeway into town, stay on it until you reach downtown, then get off and park the car as soon as you can, and get out and walk. New Orleans rivals Boston for the discomfort it causes drivers, and there are no driving routes that let you see anything you can't see better on foot—or from the St. Charles trolley. Parking in and around the French Quarter is a nightmare, and the small print on the signs can set you up for a ticket or a tow, so play it safe and park in one of many in the nearby lots, which typically charge anything from $10 a day (if you can get an Early Bird rate) to $10 an hour (if you can't).

Hwy-23: To the Gulf

From downtown New Orleans, if you really, really want to follow the Mississippi River all the way to its mouth at the Gulf of Mexico, you can. (Well, almost . . .) From the Superdome, take the US-90 bridge south across the river to Gretna, where you can join the Belle Chasse Highway (Hwy-23), which follows alongside the river for about 75 miles, ending up at Venice, still a dozen miles from the Gulf, on the fringes of the Delta National Wildlife refuge. Apart from swamps and giant freighters, the main sight along the route is old **Fort Jackson,** six miles northeast of Venice. Built following the War of 1812 to help protect the river from invasion, Fort Jackson was flooded and badly damaged by the Hurricane Katrina storm surge.

Because the Mississippi in its natural, pre-Corps state created a raised channel for itself between embankments of silt, the river sits higher than a third of Louisiana. Much of New Orleans, as the world learned during the **Hurricane Katrina** disaster, is below sea level, and the river has been dredged to a depth of more than 200 feet.

104

Index

Photo and Illustration Credits

All vintage postcards, photographs and maps in this book from the private collection of Jamie Jensen, unless otherwise credited.

Photos © Jamie Jensen: pages 12, 21, 23, 61, 86

United States Quarter-Dollar Coin Images
State quarter-dollar coin images from the United States Mint. Used with permission.

United States Postage Stamps

Pages 7, 21, 28, 38, 66, 72, 92 Greetings from America Series Stamp Designs © 2002 United States Postal Service; page 74 Tennessee Williams © 1995 United States Postal Service. Reproduction of the Tennessee Williams postage stamp by special permission of the U.S. Postal Service, Michael Deas, and The University of the South, Sewanee, Tennessee; page 81 Teddy Bears © 1998 United States Postal Service. Reproduction of the Teddy Bear stamp by special permission of the U.S. Postal Service and Gund, Inc.

Additional Credits:
Pages 9 © Mississippi River Parkway; 11 courtesy of Adam Rademacher/ This Old Farm; 13 © Turner Entertainment; 17 courtesy of the Cradle of Aviation Museum; 20 © http://www.flickr.com/photos/mulad; 24 La Crosse Lager® is a registered trademark of City Brewery, La Crosse WI; 26 courtesy of Kevin Roe Collection; 41 © Quad Cities CVB; 48 © Quincy CVB; 50 © 2006 Jupiter Images; 53 © Calhoun Ferry Company; 65 © Metropolis Convention & Visitors Bureau; 67 Memphis Convention and Visitor's Bureau; 69 © http://www.flickr.com/photos/ kevinwburkett/2322299779; 70 © http://www.flickr.com/photos/ilove memphis/4047300307; 76 © Kap Stann; 81 © Doug Pappas; 87 © Mississippi State Division of Tourism; 91 © Karl Bremer; 94, 102 © Louisiana Office of Tourism

Cover Images:
Cover postcards from the private collections of Domini Dragoone, Jamie Jensen, and Kevin Roe. For original publisher information, see *Road Trip USA,* 5th edition (Avalon Travel, 2009).

Ready to hit the open road?

Visit **roadtripusa.com** for trip ideas, maps, road trip routes, a Driver's Almanac of monthly trip suggestions, and more.

Web-exclusive features include Jamie Jensen's Road Tripper blog and free downloadable podcasts.

roadtripusa.com—the online source for road trippers!

www.moon.com

DESTINATIONS | ACTIVITIES | BLOGS | MAPS | BOOKS

MOON.COM is ready to help plan your next trip! Filled with fresh trip ideas and strategies, author interviews, informative travel blogs, a detailed map library, and descriptions of all the Moon guidebooks, Moon.com is all you need to get out and explore the world—or even places in your own backyard. While at Moon.com, sign up for our monthly e-newsletter for updates on new releases, travel tips, and expert advice from our on-the-go Moon authors. As always, when you travel with Moon, expect an experience that is uncommon and truly unique.

MOON IS ON FACEBOOK—BECOME A FAN!
JOIN THE MOON PHOTO GROUP ON FLICKR

ROAD TRIP USA
Great River Road
1st Edition

Jamie Jensen

Avalon Travel
a member of the Perseus Books Group
1700 Fourth Street
Berkeley, CA 94710, USA
www.avalontravelbooks.com

Printing History
1st edition — April 2010
5 4 3 2 1

Printed in the United States by RR Donnelley

ISBN: 978-1-59880-581-9
ISSN: 2152-3681

Editors: Kevin McLain, Elizabeth Hollis Hansen
Copy Editor: Valerie Sellers Blanton
Graphics Coordinator: Jane Musser
Production Coordinator: Darren Alessi
Map Editor: Mike Morgenfeld
Cartographers: Mike Morgenfeld, Kat Bennett
Proofreaders: Kia E. Wang, Nikki Iokimedes
Indexer: Judy Hunt

Although every effort was made to ensure that the information was correct at the time of going to press, the author and publisher do not assume and hereby disclaim any liability to any party for any loss or damage caused by errors, omissions, or any potential travel disruption due to labor or financial difficulty, whether such errors or omissions result from negligence, accident, or any other cause.